INTERVIEWING USERS,
2nd Edition
HOW TO UNCOVER COMPELLING INS

Steve Portigal

NEW YORK   2023

Interviewing Users, 2nd Edition

How to Uncover Compelling Insights

By Steve Portigal

Rosenfeld Media, LLC

125 Maiden Lane

New York, New York 10038

USA

On the Web: www.rosenfeldmedia.com

Please send errata to: errata@rosenfeldmedia.com

Publisher: Louis Rosenfeld

Managing Editor: Marta Justak

Interior Layout: Danielle Foster

Cover Design: Heads of State

Illustrator: Danielle Foster

Indexer: Marilyn Augst

Proofreader: Sue Boshers

ISBN: 1-959029-78-9

ISBN 13: 978-1-959029-78-6

LCCN: 2023943762

Printed and bound in the United States of America

This book is dedicated to the user researcher in us all—
the part of ourselves that looks at the world with curiosity,
wonders why things are the way they are, asks questions,
listens closely, and dreams about how things might be better.

HOW TO USE THIS BOOK

Who Should Read This Book?

This book is for everyone who needs to learn from people (users, customers, citizens, community members, and so on) so that what they put into the world (products, services, marketing, advertising, content, whatever) is the best that it can be. Sure, that absolutely includes user researchers, but also a lot of folks who get called "people who do research." In tech, this includes designers, engineers, marketers, product managers, and strategists.

If you've never talked to users, this book will guide you through the process of planning and executing a successful user research study. If you've been doing something "user-research-y," but haven't had any formal training, this book will provide you with some very detailed best practices for studying people. And if you've been interviewing users for a while, this book offers many opportunities for you to reflect on your own best practices.

What's in This Book?

Chapter 1, "Interviewing Addresses a Business Need," sets the stage, looking at why you learn about users, and it offers a framework for articulating the business and research needs.

Chapter 2, "Research Logistics," describes the steps to prepare for a user research study, such as finding participants and preparing your questions.

Chapter 3, "Contextual Methods—More Than Just Asking Questions," introduces a range of methods that can enhance your interviews, including artifacts you prepare and take with you, activities you ask participants to engage in, or materials you develop together with them.

Chapter 4, "The Successful Fieldwork Experience," describes how to manage the roles of the team in the field, as well as the different stages that most interviews go through, and how to prepare for and respond to those stages.

Chapter 5, "Best Practices for Interviewing," defines an overall approach—a way of being—for interviewing. All the tactical best practices emerge from this framework.

Chapter 6, "The Intricacies of Asking Questions," gets into the details of asking questions, with positive and negative examples that illustrate the impact of your word choices, phrasing, and silence.

Chapter 7, "Better Interviews," looks at common variations, typical challenges, and how to improve as an interviewer.

Chapter 8, "Documenting the Interview," reviews how to capture all the data from interviews, the limitations (and unique strengths) of taking notes, and the necessity of a proper recording.

Chapter 9, "Making Sense of Your Data," walks you through what to do with all that data and how to deliver the results.

Finally, Chapter 10, "Making an Impact with Your Research," looks at the practices, process, and infrastructure that help research results inform the decisions and actions of the rest of the organization most effectively.

What's New in the Second Edition?

This edition features two new chapters: one about analysis and synthesis and sharing research results, and another about ensuring that your user research efforts will have an impact on your organization. There are seven new short essays (we call them sidebars) from guest contributors. Plus, you'll find updated examples, stories, tips for leading interviews, and new sections about bias, remote research, ResearchOps, planning research, and research logistics.

What Comes with This Book?

This book's companion website (rosenfeldmedia.com/books/ interviewing-users-second-edition) contains a blog and additional content. The book's diagrams and other illustrations are available under a Creative Commons license (when possible) for you to download and include in your own presentations. You can find these on Flickr at www.flickr.com/photos/rosenfeldmedia/sets/.

FREQUENTLY ASKED QUESTIONS

Why is this even a book? Isn't this really just talking to people? I already know how to do that!

To actually learn something new requires interviewing, not just chatting. Unskilled interviewing leads to inaccurate and misleading information that can take your business in the wrong direction. This practice is a skill that can be fundamentally different than what you normally do in conversation. Great interviewers leverage their natural style of interacting with people, but make deliberate, specific choices about what to say, when to say it, how to say it, and when to say nothing. Doing this well is hard and takes years of practice. Chapter 6, "The Intricacies of Asking Questions," is devoted to techniques for asking questions.

Wait, is this book about interviewing or about user research?

User research is the larger practice, and interviewing is a particular method. It's a particularly powerful method because you can combine it with many other research approaches. Learning how to interview prepares you with foundational skills in listening and asking questions that can be valuable in other methods as well. In Chapter 1, "Interviewing Addresses a Business Need," and Chapter 2, "Research Logistics," I look at planning user research while Chapter 3, Contextual Methods—More Than Just Asking Questions," is about how different methods can be combined with interviewing users.

We don't have time in our development process to interview our users, so what should we do?

Sometimes "we don't have time" is a more rational-seeming way of saying "we don't need to." A strong product vision is important, but understanding what that vision means when it leaves your bubble is make-or-break stuff. In Chapter 1, I examine the impact that interviewing has on project teams. Meanwhile, gathering insights can be an organizational asset that you assemble on an ongoing basis to feed into all aspects of product development, marketing, and so on. Once you have a baseline, subsequent research can efficiently enhance and expand that body of knowledge. I'm constantly impressed by people I meet who are so hungry to bring user information into their work that they find ways to do whatever they can. In Chapter 10, "Making an Impact with Your Research," I discuss the trade-offs when time is the constraining resource.

Which team members should interview users?

While organizations are staffing a research role early in their evolution, many companies have a lot of people who talk to customers in some form. There's even a term for those folks: "people who do research." As companies need more and more insights from interviewing users, research leaders shift from struggling for acceptance to being overwhelmed by demand. It's not unusual to see them scaling up their own teams, working with outside partners, and training the rest of the organization to be better researchers themselves. Ultimately, who shouldn't be interviewing users? There will always be a range of strengths in interviewing skills; it absolutely is a specialized function, but user research is something that everyone can and should participate in. In most cases, this will exclude functions unrelated to key aspects of the business, but given the cultural value of understanding the customer, everyone could be involved in consuming the results of interviewing users, even if they aren't directly speaking to those users themselves. In Chapter 4, "The Successful Fieldwork Experience," I look at how to manage a team composed of seasoned interviewers and less-savvy colleagues.

We interviewed users and didn't learn anything new. How could that have happened?

Sometimes it's perfectly appropriate to minimize risk by validating what you already believe or by confirming that the findings from previous research still hold true. But when stakeholders report they didn't hear anything that they didn't know already, that can be a symptom of something else. Were stakeholders fully involved in outlining the research goals? Did the researchers gather an in-depth understanding of what these stakeholders already believed and what additional burning questions they had? Did the team fully dig into the research data enough to pull out more nuanced insights. Finally, if customers are still expressing the same needs they've expressed before, it begs the question, "Why haven't we done something about that?" In Chapter 1, I discuss working with stakeholders to align on business and research objectives, and in Chapter 9, "Making Sense of Your Data," I look at how to make sense of the research data beyond summarizing what people told you.

CONTENTS

At its core, user research centers the human experience. To uncover and understand those experiences, interviewing stands as one of the best methods in a UX researcher's toolkit. In this book, Steve Portigal weaves together a wonderful narrative for user interviews as a means to get as close as possible to the user, enabling us to hear directly from them about their desires, expectations, and what they need—or are willing to put up with—to get things done. (See Steve's discussion of *satisficing* as a reminder that researchers often over-index on identifying *pain points* they believe must be addressed at all costs!)

So, what do we get from talking to people? First, user interviews don't happen in a bubble. We start with a research plan that is guided by an underlying objective designed to help us ask the right questions. By asking the right questions, we uncover meaningful insights and elevate our understanding of the user experience in context. This is where we share the plan with partners to build buy-in and ensure alignment on the objective before moving too far along.

Second, connecting our deep understanding of human experience (from well-planned and well-conducted interviews) to actionable insights is key, and it's what ultimately helps us make sound decisions. The through line—from uncovering research results to recommending actionable insights—is a way of using research to deliver business impact. This is why Steve's newest edition of *Interviewing Users* is so important. Even expertly designed qualitative user research can fail to get traction if it doesn't consider strategic implications for the business.

We could describe the value of research interviews as a three-act play: **Act I**: *What is it?* **Act II**: *Is it so?* and **Act III**: *So what?* In Act I, we identify the problem we are solving and line up the right questions to ask users to better understand the world as they see it. It's in Act II that we start to look for patterns that we learned through the interview results, in order to uncover and share insights with partners for a better understanding of the user experience. Finally, in Act III, we connect those user insights to the actionable next steps by sharing our recommendations. Our focus here is making the insights actionable, starting with the user.

In this second edition, Steve skillfully directs us through each of these acts by laying a foundation of good research and interview methodology that aligns to the business. Only then does he build in sound data management and user protections (an important part of *all* research programs) through appropriate disclosures and policy. Finally, Steve provides tips and tricks for doing it all well (for example, scheduling interviews so they are close together geographically, if you are traveling locally). His perspective will help you realize why your qualitative research isn't driving business value and what to do about it. In our ever-growing quest to provide superior user experiences, this text will leave you saying, *Encore!*

—Jamika D. Burge, Ph.D.
Research leader, tech entrepreneur, and executive

INTRODUCTION

It's been a joy to revisit *Interviewing Users* ten years after writing the first edition. I've had ten more years of running interviews with users and ten more years of teaching people to do user research. I've made interesting mistakes, observed how other people succeed or struggle, and broadly reflected on my own approaches. My work has expanded into helping organizations build successful user research practices.

Over those ten years, the user research profession has cultivated an entire discipline focused on the operations of user research. The ongoing discussion about who actually does user research has been taken up under the (absolutely totally nonbiased) heading of "democratization." We're talking (more than we used to, at least) about diversity, equity, and inclusion among researchers and research participants. And throughout a years-long global pandemic, a majority of knowledge work has been conducted from our homes.

In this updated version of *Interviewing Users*, I've worked to offer more complete guidance about user research and interviewing users with these changes in mind.

Still, as society, technology, and industry evolve, other challenges for user research will emerge. For example, new environments, like virtual reality (which isn't actually new but is not yet mainstream) raise questions about how to conduct research about that environment and in that environment. Currently, there's uncertainty about AI (artificial intelligence) and what it could mean for different bits of the user research process (there's no shortage of opinions, but I'll refer you to screenwriter William Goldman who wrote *Nobody Knows Anything*). And of course, we can assume that people doing research will continue to be under pressure to move quickly, even though the greatest value comes from investing time and engaging collaboratively with each other. We must choose wisely when and how to resist the demands for so-called efficiency, so we can make sure we're getting to the good stuff.

Interviewing users is necessarily challenging, and I wrote this second edition to help us do our best work in the face of current and future challenges. I passionately believe that this is crucial work, and I'm confident that you'll find value in this book.

—Steve Portigal
August 3, 2023, Montara, California

Interviewing Addresses a Business Need

A few years back, I worked with a company that had the notion to turn a commodity safety product—the hard hat—into a premium product. They would incorporate advanced features and then charge a higher price point. I don't actually know where their idea came from, but one can imagine that they had seen all kinds of everyday products be reformulated to generate a higher scale of profit (think about Starbucks, gourmet salt, smartphones, Vitamix blenders, or horsehair mattresses). They sketched out a set of features that would improve the functional performance of the hard hat.

When I interviewed people who wore hard hats for work, I didn't ask them to evaluate the features my client had been considering. Instead, I asked them generally about their work, so I was able to uncover insight into the most significant aspects of their experience. What they were concerned about fell into an entirely different category. They talked about leaving the job site to get lunch (for example) and how awkward they felt among other people while dressed in their prominent, brightly colored safety equipment. Indeed, makers of other safety equipment like bicycling helmets, safety footwear, and safety goggles had already redesigned their products to echo fashionable caps, boots, and sunglasses, suggesting this concern was being felt broadly.

If there were to be a TEDx version of this story, then this team would have become very excited about this new and surprising area of opportunity, despite it being different from what they had already invested in (financially, intellectually, and even emotionally). They'd have torn up those plans, drawn up new ones, and eventually raked in the dough. But you know that isn't really how these things play out! In these interviews, we uncovered a significant business risk in pursuing their existing idea, so they stopped product development for their hard hat with extra functionality. On the other hand, these interviews identified another opportunity: to produce a hard hat that would address the issue of social performance. That wouldn't have fit with their organization's technical or cultural competencies, so they chose to avoid the business risk of developing a fashionable hard hat. What we learned from these interviews informed their decision not to bring any product to market.

When you get down to it, *that's* what we do as user researchers: We gather information about users in order to inform critical decisions about design, product, or other parts of the business or organization. To do this means that we go to people's homes, their offices, wherever *their* context is. We ask what they do. We ask them to show us. We get stories and long answers where we don't always know what the point is. We want them to explain everything about their world to us. People may not have a ready answer as to why they do something, but we have to listen for why. We have to ask follow-up questions and probe and infer to try to understand, for ourselves, just why something is happening the way it is. We make sense of this disparate information and show the way to act on what we've learned.

Interviewing is a specific method in user research to accomplish these goals. (*User research* is also referred to by other terms such as *design research, user experience research*, or *UXR*.) This book is about interviewing users (also referred to variously as *site visits, contextual research*, or *ethnographic research*[1]) as a method to conduct user research, so beyond an in-depth examination of best practices for interviewing users, we'll also consider user research in general. And we'll also look at other user research methods that can be integrated and combined with interviews.

Nomenclature aside, the broad outline for interviewing users is:

- Thoughtfully planning out objectives, who we'll interview, and how we'll go about it
- Deeply studying people, ideally in their context
- Exploring not only their behaviors, but also the meaning behind those behaviors
- Making sense of the data using inference, interpretation, analysis, and synthesis
- Using those insights to point toward a design, service, product, or other solution

---

1 *Ethnography* (or *ethnographic research*) can be a contentious term. If you refer to this work by that term, someone may insist that it is the wrong term. Agree that they are right and move on!

Learning About Users to Inform Decisions

Typically, when you interview people, you visit your users in their homes, their offices, their cars, their parks, and so on. But this isn't always the case. When planning a project, ask yourself if it's more insightful to bring participants in to see *your* stuff (say, prototypes you've set up in a facility meeting room) than it is for you to go out and see *their* stuff. Overall, your objective is to learn something profoundly new. (There are situations where quickly obtained, albeit shallow, information is beneficial,[2] but that's not what we'll focus on here.)

> **NOTE** EVERY ORGANIZATION CAN BENEFIT FROM RESEARCH
>
> Sometimes, companies declare that they don't need to do user research. What they typically mean is that they don't need to do *generative* user research (learning about people in order to identify product opportunities), but they are probably doing *evaluative* user research (testing the thing they are developing to make sure it's usable by people). Denying the value of generative research (because, as they might say, people don't know what they want and it's the company's mission to invent that anyway) belies a poor understanding of how user research is conducted and applied. For one thing, it's not simply asking people "what they want."
>
> For another, it's not credible that they possess an innate talent for building stuff that people love. Even if they themselves are users of the snowboards, photography equipment, or mixing gear that they make, they will choose and use those solutions differently than someone who is not inside their industry. They will be blind to differences in income, access, use cases, and so on. And they will have difficulty expanding their offering in an innovative way, because they are stuck in this model of being the user.

---

2 In "Be More Certain," Gregg Bernstein's presentation at User Research London (https://youtu.be/M1hAOCKqpSE?t=1169), he describes running a survey for only one hour and getting only 73 responses (out of thousands of users). Yet, this was sufficient to answer their key, and immediate, question: the best label to describe a specific web page element.

Often, the stated goal of interviewing users is to uncover their *pain points*. This approach mistakenly characterizes research with users as a sort of foraging activity, where if you take the effort to leave your office and enter some environment where users congregate, you'll be headed home with a heap of fresh needs. You can observe that people are struggling with X and frustrated by Y, so all you have to do is fix X and Y, and then all will be good.

Although this may be better than nothing, a lot of important information gets left behind. Insights don't simply leap out at you. You need to work hard and dig for them, which takes planning and deliberation. Further complicating the foraging model is that what people in problem-solving professions (such as designers and engineers) see as "pain points" aren't necessarily that painful for people. The term *satisficing*, coined by Herbert Simon in 1956 (combining *satisfy* and *suffice*), refers to people's tolerance—if not overall embracing—of "good-enough" solutions.

Once while settling in for a long flight, I noticed that a passenger in the row in front of me had fashioned a crude sling for their iPhone using the plastic bag that the airplane blanket came in. They had twisted the bag into a makeshift "rope," which they looped around the body of the iPhone and then jammed behind the latch that kept the tray table closed. They now had a (slightly askew) solution for watching their own device for the duration of the flight. Initially, I was critical of the ugly, inelegant result. But eventually, I realized it was beautiful in its own way—it was fashioned from the materials they had on hand. Since then, I've seen other examples of passengers making their own viewing solutions, and I've made a point of taking a picture. (See Figure 1.1 where the passenger has made an iPhone viewer out of the airline's credit card brochure and some beverage napkins.)

FIGURE 1.1
An airplane passenger viewing stand, made from the materials found on board.

Contrast these good-enough solutions with a more purpose-built accessory (see Figure 1.2): the passenger would have to have known about it, purchased it, remembered to bring it, and carried it with them. Of course, the ideal solution—not just the raw materials—would be provided by the airline itself (see Figure 1.3).

FIGURE 1.2
TabletHookz is an accessory designed specifically to hold a mobile device in an airplane seatback for hands-free inflight viewing.

FIGURE 1.3
A device holder built into the airplane seat-back allows passengers to watch videos on their own devices.

There have long been spaces online that exhibit samples of makeshift solutions. They are meant to amuse, but usually with a good measure of judgment and schadenfreude (this is the internet after all!). A good exercise for a user researcher is to seek out those images and reflect on what aspects of these solutions are successful for the people who implemented them.

I encounter satisficing in every research project: a computer desktop with an unfiled document icon in each element of the grid, an overflowing drawer of mismatched food container lids, a not-yet-unwrapped car manual, and tangled, too-short cables connecting products are all "good-enough" examples of satisficing. In other words, people find the pain of this putative problem to be less acute than the effort required by them to solve it. What you observe as a *need* may actually be something that your customer is perfectly tolerant of. Would they like all their food in containers matched with the right lids? Of course. But are they going to make much effort to accomplish that? Probably not.

Beyond simply gathering data, interviewing customers is tremendous for driving *reframes*, which are crucial shifts in perspective that flip an initial problem on its head. These new frameworks, which come from rigorous analysis and synthesis of your data, are critical. They can point the way to significant, previously unrealized possibilities for design and innovation. Even if innovation (whatever you consider that to be) isn't your goal, these frames also help you understand where (and why) your solutions will likely fail and where they will hopefully succeed. To that end, you can (and should!) interview users at different points in the development process. Here are some situations where interviewing can be valuable:

- As a way to identify new opportunities before you know what could be designed.
- To refine design hypotheses when you have some ideas about what will be designed.
- To redesign and relaunch existing products and services when you have history in the marketplace.

GAINING INSIGHT VS. PERSUADING THE ORGANIZATION

While doing ethnographic research in Japan, I accompanied my clients as they conducted an unrelated study. They brought users into a facility and showed them elegantly designed forms for printer ink cartridges. They were smooth, teardrop shapes that were shiny and coated with the color of the ink. They also showed users the current ink cartridge design: black blocks with text-heavy stickers.

Can you guess what the research revealed? Of course. People loved the new designs, exclaiming enthusiastically and caressing the shapes. Regardless of method, there was no insight to be gained here. I've gone back and forth about whether this was *good research* or *bad research*. It didn't reveal new information, but it provided tangible evidence for the organization. This team's approach suggested that there were other issues with the design process (perhaps that leaders wouldn't make decisions without supporting data from users) and while their research might have been the best way to move their process forward, ideally it wasn't the best use of a research study. ▪

A High-Level Research Plan

The operational aspects of interviewing users will be covered in the next chapter ("Research Logistics"), but here let's consider the three (plus one special guest) elements of a high-level plan. And by "plan," it's less about how you document the plan and more about the thinking that makes for an effective research project. A plan should summarize the project as you understand it at the time, including the *business problem*, the *research questions*, and the agreed-upon *research method*. Reviewing this plan with your team will ensure that you are aligned, with an opportunity to clarify, reprioritize, or expand the work.

NOTE THE ANSWER TO A NEVER-ENDING STORY

This book defaults to considering research as projects that have a beginning and an ending. But there are other models. Rolling research is a way of providing designers with regular access to participants who can provide feedback on whatever they are working on. Typically, a small number of participants are scheduled on a weekly basis. Designers and researchers determine earlier in that week what they'll show to the participants, and what questions they'll ask. Continuous discovery involves the entire product team, through the entire development cycle, and includes designing, prototyping, and getting feedback from users.

Even if you are interviewing users through one of these approaches, most of the guidance in this book (for instance, Chapter 6, "The Intricacies of Asking Questions") will apply directly.

The Business Problem

The *business problem* (or *business objective*) is what your organization—the producer of products, services, solutions, and so on—is faced with, as shown in Table 1.1.

TABLE 1.1 BUSINESS PROBLEM EXAMPLES

Business Problem
We're sunsetting a legacy product and replacing it with one that uses a different technology.
Our new product didn't do as well as we had hoped.
We want to move into a new market.
A new competitor is taking some of our market share.
We're roadmapping what new features we'll be developing for our current service.
Product feedback is strong but repeat orders are low.

To get an in-depth understanding of the business problem, you'll probably want to talk with your stakeholders. You'll learn more about this topic in Chapters 2 and 10, "Making an Impact with Your Research."

UNCOVER MISALIGNMENT EARLY

I once worked with a client who made a digital platform used for particularly complex transactions. They already supported the buyers, sellers, and their respective brokers, and now were looking at opportunities to incorporate the other entities (known as "third parties") in these transactions. This research was a strategic priority, traceable to goals assigned from on high.

To kick off the project, we scheduled two activities (loosely based on the Questions Workshop[3]) with different groups of stakeholders. We set up a spreadsheet to capture decisions they were planning to make and what information about these other users would help in making those decisions. In the first workshop, the main project sponsor halted the proceeding to ask "Now, what do we mean by 'third parties?'" I assumed they knew, and they assumed I knew! I was surprised, but glad they weren't afraid to ask a "dumb" question. It was a disconnect, but an important one to uncover, and at the right time. We aligned on a definition and then moved forward with the questions. In the second workshop, a stakeholder kicked off the session by telling us "Just so you know, we're already coding a solution." Again, I was surprised, but this was very helpful to understand at the outset rather than later. ■

The Research Question

The research question identifies the information you need from users to provide guidance about the business problem. Whereas the business problem looks inward, the research question looks outward—in other words, the business problem is about *you* and the research question is about *your users* (see Table 1.2).

Sometimes the research questions are clustered and nested. For example, the business problem "We are investing heavily in social media and want our customers to promote our services more" might lead to this set of research questions.

- What do people's social networks look like? What tools do they use and how are their networks structured?
  - How are purchase decisions driven by the structure of people's social network (on and offline)?
  - How do people leverage social networks for shopping and other kinds of decision-making? Who has influence with them currently?

---

3   Created by Sinéad Davis Cochrane. See the details at www.researchstrategy .info/_files/ugd/883140_8f3d7b2226374acd98cc7b498fd64bd0.pdf

- Who among their social network (and beyond) are trusted sources of information for various decisions and purchases (particularly within the client's area of business)?

TABLE 1.2 RESEARCH QUESTION EXAMPLES

Business Problem	Research Question
We're sunsetting a legacy product and replacing it with one that uses a different technology.	What platform-specific aspects of the experience are important to customers?
Our new product didn't do as well as we had hoped.	Were our assumptions about what people wanted to see in the product correct? Did the product deliver on that?
We want to move into a new market.	How do these users do this activity? What tools do they use? What is important to them?
A new competitor is taking some of our market share.	What do users of our competitor's product like about it? Why are they choosing it?
We're roadmapping what new features we'll be developing for our current service.	How well can people accomplish their goals with this new design?
Product feedback is strong but repeat orders are low.	What are the highs and lows for people using the product from start to finish?

To further inform the research questions, you should review previous research reports, existing products, and in-development prototypes. Look for relevant research findings, explicitly stated assumptions or hypotheses, and implicit hypotheses in the decisions that have already been made.

When I ask teams to work on articulating their business problems and research questions, they often find it surprisingly challenging, but also enlightening. There won't be a singular perfect answer, but the process of considering the specifics is valuable for developing a deeper intention and focus for the research. That process might include going back and forth on different variations and wordings. It might not produce a perfectly structured 1:1 relationship between the business problem and the research question. If you practice with a colleague, before long, you'll have a feel for the right level of granularity and structure for you.

You should also conduct interviews with your stakeholders—they are often consumers of the research findings who are less likely to be involved in the day-to-day study. I typically aim for 6–8 stakeholders, although some clients ask for twice that amount. These are one-on-one conversations that run between 30 and 60 minutes and are used to dig deeper into objectives and set the stage for working collaboratively. Many of the interview techniques in this book (such as what I'll cover in Chapter 5, "Best Practices for Interviewing") apply to interviewing stakeholders, although you may find it less comfortable to ask "dumb" questions if you feel your credibility could be at stake. You should ask the stakeholders about the following:[4]

- Their history with the organization and the research topic
- Business objectives for the project and specific questions the research should answer
- Current beliefs about the customer, the user, and the proposed solution
- Organizational or other barriers to be mindful of
- Concerns or uncertainty around the method

Even though what you learn will undoubtedly inform all of the activities throughout the project, the immediate output is the research questions—articulating what you want to learn from the interviews.

---

4   See a sample stakeholder interview guide at https://portigal.com/stakeholder-guide

With the overall goal of trying to understand the problem space you're exploring, gathering the language that is used to talk about that problem space, and planning what you're going to ask your research participants, there are other activities that you can do at this point. Secondary research (also called *desk research*) gives you a sense of current and historical thinking through what's been written about your topic already. Look at the mainstream press, the business press, academic papers, internal or external corporate reports, blogs, online forums, newsletters, books, and so on. Identify industry, academic, or other experts and interview them. You may also seek out a few experiences that will give you some perspective on the topic. Look at similar products and how they are being sold online or in retail. Try an experience yourself.

For a project that sought to understand how our client could facilitate a more emotional connection with their customers, we visited a handful of environments that had reputations for successfully bonding with their users (an Apple store; Powell's Books in Portland, OR; the dog-friendly Fort Funston in San Francisco; a Wawa convenience store in Philadelphia; and Rainbow Grocery in San Francisco) and observed the environment, the people that were there, and hypothesized about what factors were either leveraging or contributing to the relationship. This led to topics to explore in the interviews and examples to compare and contrast with during the analysis stage.

The Research Method

The research method is how you will gather the information needed to answer the research question. Here are a few examples of user research methods (other than interviewing):

- **Usability testing:** Typically done in a controlled environment, such as a lab, users interact with a product (or a prototype or simulation), and various factors (time to complete a task, error rate, preference for alternate solutions) are measured.

- **A/B testing:** This type of testing compares the effectiveness of two different versions of the same design (e.g., advertisement, website landing page) by launching them both under similar circumstances.

- **Quantitative survey:** A questionnaire, primarily using closed-ended questions, is distributed to a larger sample in order to obtain statistically significant results.

- **Web analytics:** Measurement and analysis of various data points are obtained from Web servers, tracking cookies, and so on. Aggregated over a large number of users, Web analytics can highlight patterns in navigation, user types, the impact of day and time on usage, and so on.

- **Focus group:** This is a moderated discussion with 4 to 12 participants in a research facility, often used to explore preferences (and the reasons for those preferences) among different solutions.

- **Central location test:** In a market research facility, groups of 15 to 50 people watch a demo and complete a survey to measure their grasp of the concept, the appeal of various features, the desirability of the product, and so on.

Of course, researchers make up new methods regularly. (See more about methods in Chapter 3, "Contextual Methods—More Than Just Asking Questions.")

Selecting an Appropriate Method

In the aptly named "When to Use Which User-Experience Research Methods" by Christian Rohrer,[5] the article organizes some of the more common methods into a framework. (Does the method look at people's behaviors or their attitudes? Is the method qualitative or quantitative? Does the method look at someone's use of a product?) (See Figure 1.4.) The article provides guidance about which methods are best suited for different contexts. For example, if the goal of the research is to find new directions and opportunities, then the best methods (according to Rohrer) include diary studies, interviews, surveys, participatory design, and concept testing.

---

5 Christian Rohrer, "When to Use Which User-Experience Research Methods," *Nielsen Norman Group* (blog), July 17, 2022, www.nngroup.com/articles/which-ux-research-methods/

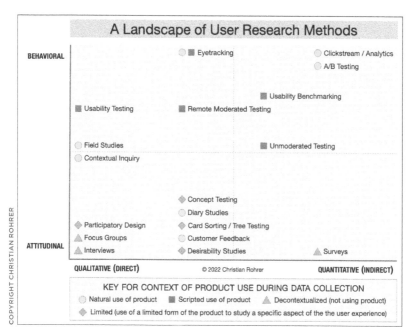

FIGURE 1.4

Christian Rohrer's "Landscape" organizes user research methods by behavior/attitude and quantitative/qualitative.

NOTE MARKET RESEARCH AND USER RESEARCH

In some companies, market research is a separate department from user research and may even report to different leaders.[6] It also seems like a different career path; people find their way to either discipline from different backgrounds. But what's the difference? It's common—but wildly inaccurate—to attempt to distinguish the two by the methods used (market research does focus groups and surveys; user research does interviews and usability testing) or the objectives (market research looks at attitudes and user research observes behavior). Figure 1.4 invites us to consider a bigger picture—a broad set of methods and objectives that no one discipline "owns" exclusively.

---

6 Kathryn Campbell, then at Ticketmaster, used a model from Forrester, the Insight Center of Excellence, to set up a team that incorporated both market research and user research. Steve Portigal, "29: Kathryn Campbell of Ticketmaster," *Dollars to Donuts* (podcast), March 28, 2020, https://portigal.com/podcast/29-kathryn-campbell-of-ticketmaster/

Taking a different approach, Sam Ladner developed a guide shown in Figure 1.5 that recommends a research method based on where your product is in its lifecycle.

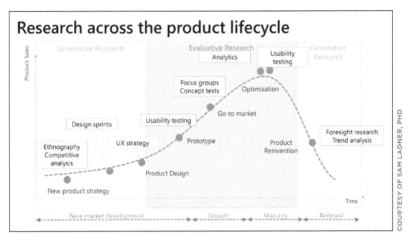

Research across the product lifecycle

FIGURE 1.5
Sam Ladner organizes user research methods by the maturity stage of the product's sales.

Combining User Research Methods

Interviewing can be used in combination with other techniques. *Mixed methods* refer to combining multiple methods (typically qualitative and quantitative) together in one study. I've used an exploratory interviewing study to identify topics for a global quantitative segmentation study. I've combined a Central Location Test (where larger groups watched a demo in a single location such as a research facility and filled out a survey) in parallel with in-home interviews to get a deeper understanding of the potential for the product. I've also mixed together different qualitative activities (say, a larger sample for a diary study, and then follow-up interviews with a subset of participants). It can be valuable to combine a set of approaches and get the advantages of each.

NOTE QUANTITATIVE USER EXPERIENCE RESEARCH

Kitty Z Xu, a quant user experience researcher, explains how this emerging discipline uses two kinds of data: *sentimental* (such as feelings, perceptions and understanding) from surveys and *behavioral* (from logging data, usage metrics and more).[7] Researchers in quant UXR make use of skills from a variety of fields, including user research, survey science, data science, and analytics. While interviewing (or qualitative user experience research) looks for insights in a small sample, quant UXR builds insights *at scale*—meaning collecting hundreds or thousands of samples that are representative of a larger population.

Choosing Interviewing

Interviewing isn't the right approach for every problem. Because it favors depth over sample size, use interviewing when you don't need statistically significant data. Being semi-structured, each interview will be unique and reveal something new about what you're trying to understand (but it can be challenging to objectively tally data points across the sample). Although you are ideally interviewing in context, you are now a participant in that environment. Sitting with users to show you how they use a website isn't supposed to be naturalistic (versus the way a tool that intercepts and observes users who visit that website captures their actual behavior).

People are not good at predicting their future behavior, especially not for brand-new, hypothetical situations (see "Manage Bias" in Chapter 4). There are bad questions and bad ways of asking questions (see Chapters 6 and 7), but you should be skeptical of broadly dogmatic interviewing advice that warns you *never* to ask about future behavior, like "How much would you pay for this?" You can definitely ask the question, but it's important to understand what you can and can't do with the answer. You won't get a number that is helpful for your pricing strategy, but you can learn about their rationale for that number or hear a thoughtful reflection about perceived value. Your questions in an interview can reveal mental models that exist today, which will be insightful for the decisions you have made, but the literal responses about future behavior probably won't be accurate.

---

7   Kitty's helpful explainers about quant UXR are at https://pinterest.design/youre-a-stem-major-your-dream-job-might-be-in-design-b3f947941360 and https://pinterest.design/what-is-quantitative-user-experience-research-at-pinterest-8eb17c69a0fc

Participant Questions

This isn't really part of the high-level plan, but it's included here because discussion about the research question sometimes drifts into specific questions that people imagine asking participants. I led a workshop with creative entrepreneurs who struggled to articulate what they wanted to learn from their interviews but were brimming over with what questions they wanted to ask. Because they really were unable to come up with research questions, our workaround was to build out the participant questions and then step back and ask what those questions were collectively in service of (in other words, the research question).

You may generate (or collect) some participant questions during this high-level planning process. Unless they are helpful in getting you unstuck on your research questions, just file them away for now. In Chapter 2, we'll focus more on the questions we plan to ask.

Aligning on the Research Plan

Since you're seeing this in a book, where the different elements of the plan (business problem, research question, and research method) are presented in sequence, you might reasonably conclude that you should also proceed linearly. First, get clarity on your business challenge, then uncover your research questions, and then choose the best method to answer those questions! Sounds good?

Ah, but it doesn't usually work that way. Depending on how a project is initiated (a prospective client generates a Request for Proposal, a stakeholder sends a request by email, and so on), it may be more or less based on one of the three. You may be asked *Here's the situation, how can research help us?* Or *We need to learn such-and-such about these users.* Or *Can we complete this method of research within this time frame?* But no matter how the conversation begins, it's up to you to fill in the rest of the pieces.

If you're given a research question, ask why that information is needed. If you're given a research method, ask what they hope to learn, and then ask why that information is needed. Sometimes, the people you're going to work with haven't thought about this, but often it's just implicit and your questions will help make it explicit. You want to make sure that not only are you and the clients or stakeholders aligned, but crucially that these different pieces are in alignment: the method has to produce the information that is needed, and the information that is needed should be in support of the actions the team plans to take.

The people who need the results of the research don't necessarily understand the range of methods and when to use them. Don't agree to use a prescribed method that doesn't align with the necessary results, because the blame will fall to you at the end when you can't deliver. Facilitating the alignment between challenge, question, and method is part of the expertise a researcher brings. People who do research should seek an experienced researcher to advise on these high-level aspects of the research plan.

To Interview Well, One Must Study

Much of the technique of interviewing is based on one of your earliest developmental skills: asking questions (see Figure 1.6). You all know how to ask questions, but if you asked questions in interviews the way you ask questions in typical interactions, you would fall short. In a conversational setting, you are perhaps striving to talk at least 50 percent of the time, and mostly to talk about yourselves. But interviewing is not a social conversation. Falling back on your social defaults is going to get you into trouble!

Interviewing users involves a special set of skills. It takes work to develop these skills. The fact that it looks like an everyday act can actually make it harder to learn how to conduct a good interview because it's easy to take false refuge in existing conversational approaches. Developing your interviewing skills is different than developing a technical skill (say, milkshake-machine recalibration) because you had nothing to fall back on when learning about milkshake machines. With interviewing, you may need to learn how to override something you already know. Think of other professionals who use verbal inquiry to succeed in their work: whether it is police officers interrogating a suspect, a lawyer cross-examining an opposing witness, or a reference librarian helping a patron, the verbal exchange is a deliberate, learned specialty that goes beyond what happens in everyday conversation. For you as an interviewer, it's the same thing.

We'll revisit improving as an interviewer in Chapter 7, "Better Interviews."

COURTESY OF CHERYL PORTIGAL-TODD, 2008

FIGURE 1.6
Childhood is marked
by frequent, inevitable
question-asking.

The Impact of Interviewing

Interviewing creates a shared bonding experience, often a galvanizing one, for the product development team (which can include researchers, designers, engineers, marketers, product management, and beyond). In addition to the information you learn from people and the inspiration you gain from meeting them, there's a whole other set of transformations you go through. You might call it *empathy*—say a more specific understanding of the experience and emotions of the customer—which might even be as simple as seeing "the user" or "the customer" as a real live person in all their glorious complexity. But what happens when people develop empathy for a series of individuals they might meet in interviews? They experience an increase in their overall capacity for empathy.[8]

---

8 William Hambleton Bishop describes a process for interactions between couples that sounds a lot like many of the best practices for judgment-free listening that I've covered here. He observes that as his clients go through this process, their overall capacity for empathy increases significantly. If we substitute user interviews for the similar process Bishop outlines, it's good evidence that we can expect our own empathy to increase as well. William Bishop, "Empathy Building Exercise—Learning to Be Empathetic—Increasing Emotional Understanding," *Thoughts from a Therapist* (blog), June 8, 2011, www.thoughtsfromatherapist.com/2011/06/08/empathy-building-exercise-learning-to-be-empathetic-increasing-emotional-understanding/

This evolution in how individual team members see themselves, their connection to their colleagues, their design work, and the world around them starts to drive shifts in the organizational culture (see Figure 1.7). This capacity for empathy is not sufficient to change a culture, but it is necessary.

FIGURE 1.7
Team experiences that are challenging and out-of-the-ordinary create goodwill and a common sense of purpose.

More tactically, these enlightened folks are better advocates for customers and better champions for the findings and implications of what has been learned in interviews.

The wonderful thing about these impacts is that they come for free (or nearly). Being deliberate in your efforts to interview users will pay tremendous dividends for your products, as well as the people who produce them.

In a Twitter thread,[9] Mollie Ruskin wrote about a civic design project, saying,

> While the research was "about" operations and staff capacity and a complex process for answering heaps of emails, I quickly found we were stumbling over a set of questions fundamental to the function of our representative democracy.

So, as much as you work to identify and align on your business problem and your research questions, that alignment is limited by the fact that the only information you have comes from before you have done any research. Mollie reminds us that our understanding of the problem (and the opportunity) can change.

The worst thing a research team can do, however, is to come back to the project sponsors and say "Welp, we know we were looking at operations and capacity but really the issue is the underpinnings of our democracy." Ideally, the broader team is collaborative enough that they will see these reframes together and can decide what to do about them. When I'm in this situation, I try to address the initial scope ("Here's what we know about the gaps in the operations and how this impacts staff capacity") and present the emergent topic as one that builds on the original goals ("and, the real issue that connects these infrastructure decisions is the very nature of our democratic processes."). If the organization isn't ready (yet) to address the larger insight (and often they won't be—just look at the size of the shift in Mollie's example!) at least they can move forward on their original problem, and you've planted the seed for a future effort. This probably won't be the last time this underlying issue emerges, and at some point, it may not be possible to ignore it any longer.

9　@mollieruskin (Molly Ruskin), "A few days ago, a big meaty project that I spent a bunch of last year working on was released to the world," Twitter, February 6. 2018, https://twitter.com/mollieruskin/status/960954942428196864

The Last Word

It's become increasingly common, perhaps even required, for companies to include user research in their design and development process. Among many different approaches to user research, interviewing (by whatever name you want to call it) is a *deep dive* into the lives of customers.

- Interviewing can be used in combination with other techniques, such as identifying key themes through interviews and then validating them quantitatively in a subsequent study.

- At a distance, interviewing looks just like the everyday act of talking to people, but interviewing well is a real skill that takes work to develop.

- Interviewing can reveal new "frames" or models that flip the problem on its head. These new ways of looking at the problem are crucial to identifying new, innovative opportunities.

- Interviewing can be used to help identify what could be designed, to help refine hypotheses about a possible solution that is being considered, or to guide the redesign of an existing product that is already in the marketplace.

- Teams who share the experience of meeting their users are enlightened, aligned, and more empathetic.

CHAPTER 2

Research
Logistics

A	nyone who has ever painted a room knows all too well the amount of time it takes to prepare before you ever brush a single stroke. You have to select a paint color, type, and finish; acquire the paint, brushes, rollers, and other supplies; tape off windows and trim; move the furniture; spread the drop cloths; and so on. Sometimes I find this preparation tedious and unrewarding (I wanna see paint on the wall!), but I also know from experience that all the prep work has a dramatic impact on the quality and efficiency of the painting process itself. I know you see this coming, but here it is: Interviewing users requires a similar amount of prep work. There is extensive preparation involved before you begin asking users anything.

In the previous chapter, you learned the foundational planning activities for a user research study: essentially who to study, what you'll do with them, and why you're doing this study in the first place. In this chapter, you'll figure out how to find participants, where/when to do the interviews, and detail all of the planning that will make your time in the field go smoothly.

As the field of user research has grown and matured, there are a growing number of tools and services to support different parts of the overall workflow.[1] The company User Interviews (itself an online tool for recruiting participants and more) has annually produced a visualization[2] of the existing tools for note-taking, transcription, analysis, surveys, recruiting, scheduling, paying incentives, recording, analyzing, and so on. The availability of these tools, often not fully mature software, has changed much of the logistics and operations for research. In-house operations people can evaluate these tools to see how they serve the needs of researchers, coordinate with IT and legal around security and compliance, and help researchers and people who do research to integrate these tools into their own workflow.

---

1   A notable moment in this trajectory was when venture capital firm Andreessen Horowitz published an analysis in 2021 noting how fragmented and poorly integrated the current set of products were—Jennifer Li, "The Market for User Research Platforms," *Andreessen Horowitz* (blog), April 6, 2021, https://a16z.com/2021/04/06/the-market-for-user-research-platforms/

2   The 2022 version is www.userinterviews.com/ux-research-tools-map-2022; while these documents are valuable, each iteration draws heavily on a cute-but-irrelevant metaphor (role-playing games, subways) that hampers readability and usability.

HOW RESEARCHOPS HELPS TURBOCHARGE RESEARCH PRACTICES

By Kate Towsey

Kate Towsey is an expert in helping organizations scale research skills, practices, and infrastructure to hundreds of people. She is the founder of the Cha Cha Club, an invite-only club for dedicated ResearchOps professionals.[3] She is widely known as the queen of ResearchOps.

In early 2018, I started the ResearchOps Community[4] to bring together a disparate group of people from around the world who, like me, were knee-deep in the job of delivering operations to support scaled-up user research. In the same year, I launched the #WhatisResearchOps project,[5] which involved hundreds of researchers from across the globe in defining *ResearchOps* (sometimes referred to as *ReOps* or *ResOps*). ResearchOps had existed in forward-thinking organizations like Microsoft, Airbnb, and Salesforce for up to two decades prior to the Community, but the #Whatis-ResearchOps framework helped give it shape and it put it on the map.

It's often assumed that the chief role of ResearchOps is to unburden researchers of the logistics of doing research. While ResearchOps should make planning tasks less demanding for researchers (because common processes are standardized, repeatable, automated, and so on), the goal of ResearchOps is to deliver the skills, infrastructure, and services that help a research organization or practice to achieve *its* goals. The focus is on supporting the needs of the collective and not the individual.

Here's a comparison to illustrate the relationship between research and ResearchOps. Someone getting in their car and driving to work is a commuter. To commute, they must maintain a car, a driver's license, the skills to drive, and they must have a good sense of direction, or a map, and the tools to view the map. For the commuter (and many other commuters) to be able to get to work efficiently, large teams of people need to be coordinated to design, build, and maintain the roadways, traffic lights, smooth flow of traffic, accurate maps that work across various platforms, and so on. The former is a researcher, the latter is research operations.

continues

---

3 https://chacha.club

4 I stepped away from leading the ResearchOps Community in 2019. It can be found at https://researchops.community/

5 Kate Towsey, "A framework for #WhatisResearchOps," *Medium*, October 24, 2018.

While a researcher has best practices for logistics and planning (as this chapter describes), ResearchOps focuses on delivering infrastructure that will support a million of the same journeys, including:

- Efficient routes to participants via agencies or panels

- Documented protocols so that researchers can easily access resources, such as briefing templates for agencies or how-to guides for recruitment platforms

- Available budget for recruitment projects so that finances don't slow a researcher down

- Supporting researchers to easily schedule research participants using tools (such as Calendly) that don't distribute personal identifiable information (PII) across calendars

- A library of legal-approved processes for NDA (nondisclosure agreement), ethical practices, and release of data to suit various cohorts of participants (say executives, versus vulnerable populations), as well as training and a documented protocol for delivering informed consent across different research contexts such as moderated and unmoderated, remote versus in the field, and so on

- Resources to support safe and effective field trips: everything from field kits to protocols for what to do if things go wrong

Finding Participants

Finding (or recruiting) participants is a crucial part of preparing for fieldwork, yet some teams treat it very casually, relying on friends and family (an approach that is sometimes justified with the "guerilla" rhetoric) or even worse, grabbing barely screened participants off the street, or in a store, or on a website (this is known as an *intercept*). More established research teams, however, have a repeatable participant recruiting process as part of ResearchOps, such as people dedicated to building pools of participants and supporting tools and infrastructure to help researchers (and PwDR) arrange for their own research participants. This can include outsourcing to third parties that provide participant panels and a range of participant recruiting and scheduling services.

- Spaces to do research in a lab or a remote platform (and the support and training for how to use them)
- Finances, protocols, and platforms to say "thank you" to research participants in satisfying, brand-building, and effective ways
- Managing data respectfully and compliantly from start to end (also known as *data governance*)
- Honoring the knowledge gained from research interviews by ensuring that it's well-stored and shared (also known as *research knowledge management*)

As the field of research has grown, and organizations seek to empower both a larger number of researchers and "people who do research" (otherwise known by the term I coined, *PwDR*), dedicated ResearchOps practices have become more common, too. There are now hundreds of people across the world who work as dedicated ResearchOps specialists, and they're continually developing specialist skills to meet the needs of the job.

For more about building Research Operations, check out my book *Research That Scales*.[6]

---

6   Kate Towsey, *Research That Scales: The Research Operations Handbook* (New York: Rosenfeld Media, to be published 2024).

Defining Criteria for Your Sample

Identifying the right group of participants (the sample) for a research project is essential. Interviewing people who don't have the desired and relevant context wastes time and challenges the credibility of your work. You will always have recruiting failures or interviews that don't quite work out as hoped, but your planning efforts can help limit their frequency. The first step (sometimes this takes place early on, as you are scoping a project) is to identify the key characteristics for your sample. For example:

- Six households who regularly use a meal kit service:
  - Mix of urban, suburban, and rural
  - Mix of single adult households, multiple adult households, households with children
  - All between ages of 25 and 55

- Two households who rely primarily on convenience food and restaurant takeout
- Two "home chef" (or aspiring) households

A few things to note in this example:

- By looking at households with multiple people, you're looking at several parts of an experience (people who primarily prepare the food eaten by them and others, and the people who consume it); even if you are designing only one part of the experience, you can gain a deeper understanding by looking at it from multiple points of view.

- Much of these criteria will need to be defined specifically, for example what you mean by "regularly," what are acceptable examples of a meal service, what defines "urban," how you define "convenience food," what frequency of use constitutes "rely," etc.

- You can match most of these criteria with objective questions about behavior; only the idea of aspiring to be a home chef is a subjective question about attitude.

- The demographic questions are proxies for lifestyle differences that might influence your subject's behavior or preferences—for example, someone with kids probably makes dinner differently than someone living on their own, but these are all assumptions.

- *Who you learn from isn't necessarily who you build for*! You may have existing business reasons not to build a solution for someone living on their own, but you are including them in the sample to highlight the contrast between them and your target market (say, households with kids). During fieldwork and analysis, you may more clearly perceive a characteristic of one group because of something you've heard from the other group.

That last one is worth repeating: ***Who you learn from isn't necessarily who you build for.*** The bulk of your sample should probably be the people whose problems you want to solve, but you should salt-and-pepper your sample with some other kinds of people. When these other participants, who you aren't planning to build for, share their particular point of view (say, product X is useless to them because they don't have kids), that point of view highlights an attribute of the other participants who you are building for (say, product

X is useful to them because they do have kids). Sometimes you won't have realized this common characteristic of your target user because it's been right under your nose the whole time.

For example, whatever your behavior/brand/service/product is, consider adding a few people from any of the following groups:

- Non-user
- Extreme user
- Peripheral user
- Lead user
- Subject matter expert
- Wannabe user
- Should-be user
- Future user
- Past user
- Hater
- Loyal to competitor

As with the research goals, you should circulate these criteria with the project team and make sure that everyone is on the same page. Aligning on these criteria can be contentious. When teams ask themselves who their customers are (or could be), this question surfaces any number of disconnects: hypotheses masquerading as facts, aspirations, and mass hallucinations. This can surface a broader sense—*prior* to research—about who is affected by the product and who it is being designed for.

For example, in a study that was focused on online shopping for athletic apparel, we spent four weeks (of what was supposed to be a six-week project) actively negotiating, among an ever-increasing set of stakeholders, the basic archetypes of customers we should look at. It was daunting, but essential for having any success further down the road. We were not able to change the underlying cultural issues that were causing this issue (nor were we trying to), but we were able to use our expertise in planning and executing these sorts of studies to help resolve the deadlock. Although these four weeks were exhausting and frustrating, we did get the team unstuck and moved forward on the research itself.

To make your sample more inclusive,[7] researcher Megan Campos advises against "try[ing] to include absolutely every one of every identity of every level of intersectionality in every recruit," but rather you should "think about what diversity and inclusivity mean in the context of your product or experience and who you need to include who hasn't been traditionally included. Just because you're not including everyone with every study doesn't mean you can't eventually talk to everyone."[8] You can't completely address insufficient diversity with a single study, but over time—and multiple research efforts—you can broaden the set of people you are including.

Sample Size

The number of people you need to include in your research sample is an obvious question to answer in the planning stage, but it's also an elusive question to get a definitive answer to. Social science uses the term "saturation" to describe the state at which you stop learning anything new (and thus can stop doing more research). Applying this is challenging in user research settings, because you don't fully know if you're learning anything new just from the interviews themselves. You have to do analysis and synthesis (see Chapter 9, "Making Sense of Your Data") to make sense of your research data. If you aren't seeing any meaningful patterns in your data, that probably means that you need to go back and talk to more people. Of course, that can be a challenge to project timelines.

Experience (especially with any particular population or topic) helps researchers to get better at estimating what kind of sample size they need. It might depend on how many different kinds of people you want to talk to, and what kinds of topics you want to talk with them about. People who are newer to research tend to overestimate how different people are going to be from each other. If you are looking at a product or service, there can be a good chance that much of what

---

7   See also "Inclusive Research Operations," *ReOps Community Call*, November 2022, https://vimeo.com/780222440

8   Megan Campos and Dan Berlin, "Diverse Participant Recruiting Is Essential to Authentic User Research," *97 UX Things* (podcast), March 1, 2022, https://97uxthings.buzzsprout.com/1798703/10045808-megan-campos-research-diverse-participant-recruiting-is-essential-to-authentic-user-research

people experience is similar. Different types of people may react to that experience differently, but it's still a range of responses to a common topic.

Subjectively, I prefer a sample to be big enough so that as the interviews go on, there's eventually a critical mass of stuff to think about (again, see Chapter 9), but not so big that I can't keep straight the general profile and stories of everyone I've met. When I'm asked to take on a piece of work with what feels like too large a sample, I'll propose breaking that down into smaller studies that we'll run in sequence, using what we've learned in one study to inform what we ask about in the next study.

The Screener

From the criteria, you can produce a document called a *screener* (see Figure 2.1).[9] Functionally, it resembles a survey. You will determine what responses qualify as potential participants. The screener includes a mix of question types (including yes/no, multiple choice, and open-ended) and uses responses to direct the flow through the set of questions.

When writing your screening questions, keep the following advice in mind:

- Ask objective questions where it's easy for people to answer in a way that matches your intentions. "Do you regularly cook at home? [YES/NO]" relies on the potential participant's interpretation of *regularly*. "In the last week, how many dinners have you prepared at home? [NONE/1–3/4 or MORE]" is less subjective.

- You are trying to screen people into or out of the study as simply as possible. You can look at that last example and be concerned that maybe last week wasn't typical, like if they were on vacation, or they had a soccer tournament… but you aren't trying to properly segment each individual, you are trying to get your sample. Sure, if you could ask a dozen follow-up questions, you might be able to understand the context better and see if this person does indeed regularly cook at home, but you can't. The soccer tournament household is out of the study. If your population is much smaller, you'd make a different trade-off.

---

9   See the complete document at https://portigal.com/screener

- Don't reveal who you want to be in your study. "Are you 18–55 and play online word games daily?" tips your hand and allows people to misrepresent themselves in order to get into your study. Instead, use multiple-choice questions to conceal the answer you are looking for, for example:

Q1: How old are you?

- Under 18
- 18 to 25
- 26 to 40
- 41 to 55
- 55 or older

Q2: Which, if any, of the following online games do you play daily?

- First-person shooter
- Adventure or role-playing
- Word games
- Puzzles
- Other
- None

---

2. Do you own a mobile device that you use regularly to listen to music?

Yes
No   **DISMISS**

2a.. If yes, how long have you owned that mobile device?
Less than 3 months   **DISMISS**
Between 3 months and 1 year
More than 1 year

2b. If yes, how many hours per week do you estimate you listen to music on your mobile device?
IF < 5 THEN DISMISS

3. Do you listen to music on a computer or a TV?
Yes
No   **DISMISS**

3a. If yes, how often?

Daily
Weekly
Every other week   **DISMISS**
Monthly   **DISMISS**
Less than once per month   **DISMISS**

4. Do you regularly listen to music on any other devices?
Yes (describe_____)
No

5. How many music platforms do you have paid subscriptions to? Do not count platforms where you have a free subscription or that don't charge to listen.
IF < 4 THEN DISMISS

7. What online sites do you typically go to when learning about new music? Select all that apply.

RollingStone.com
Variety
Melody Maker.uk
Hot100
YouTube
USAToday
TikTok

FIGURE 2.1

An excerpt of a screener showing objective questions that screen prospective participants in or out.

Getting Participants

Once you have a finalized screener, you have to find participants. Some organizations will have a "panel"—a database of customers or users who have opted in to participate in research. Some organizations have their own database of users but haven't pulled that into a panel. In enterprise settings especially, you might have to reach out to people who own relationships (sales, account managers, and others).[10] Sometimes the support function can provide names based on who they've been in contact with. Your database may include all of the information you need to include someone in your research (such as interaction with certain features, duration as user, or location), in which case you can invite them to participate (see "Inviting People to Participate" later), but sometimes there may be further information you need to determine if they are suitable for your study. In that case, you'll have to reach out with your screener to find out their meal prep for the last week (for example).

For consumer research, I have frequently used an external market research recruiting agency. They will use our screener and their own database, or customer lists provided by our clients, or will reach out in whatever venues they can to find people. My best experiences are with agencies that I can work with closely throughout the process. At the outset, they give my screener a close reading, identify missing elements, and clarify any ambiguities. As the recruiting process proceeds, they give daily updates (even when they haven't found anyone), and they point out any criteria that are commonly eliminating otherwise good participants, in case we want to make an adjustment.

There are recruiters who specialize in specific populations like disabled participants,[11] healthcare professionals, patients, corporate executives, IT, and geographic regions.

Great recruiters will establish an initial rapport with your participants and help them feel comfortable and enthusiastic about the process. They will also support you in creating a reasonable schedule, allowing for travel time, rush-hour traffic, and so on.

---

10 People frequently encounter challenges when trying to get access to someone else's relationships. For more on the process to overcoming that resistance see Teresa Torres, "Ask Teresa: My Sales Team Won't Let Me Talk to Customers. What Now?" *Product Talk* (blog), May 18, 2022, www.producttalk.org/2022/05/sales-owns-customer-relationships/

11 Such as Fable (https://makeitfable.com/testers/) and Knowbility's Access-Works (https://knowbility.org/services/accessworks)

Recruiting Challenges

Researcher Megan Campos highlights the opportunity for more inclusive participant recruiting: "There's a huge need with recruiters to go into new communities, look into new spaces, look at creative ways of recruiting and building trust with organizations like churches and hospitals. Because otherwise, it's going to be hard to yield people who don't look the same as everyone else we've talked to."[12]

Dana Chisnell wrote about going "where our people were: streets, libraries, community centers, churches, malls" as "two middle-class, middle-aged white women wearing sensible shoes and kindly expressions and carrying clipboards."[13] They were recruiting participants whom they interviewed on the spot. Dana describes the specific recruiting practices they developed for their situation, but more broadly her work models the significant effort and commitment required when finding participants is essential but not trivial.

Many organizations face what feels like their unique participant recruiting challenge: a very small number of customers, no customers yet, a complicating aspect in the relationship between users and your company, and so on. And while there are some best practices and guidance, your exact situation will require some creativity, experimentation, and networking to find peers with similar challenges. Whatever constraints you face should drive you to adapt and compromise. Can you change the incentive? Rethink who you should be talking to? Reinvent how you want to engage with people?

Inviting People to Participate

When reaching out to people to participate in research, you should put some work into crafting the message. Try to consider your recipient's context and use relevant, appropriate language.

- The default formality of using your title may not be necessary. Does your audience know what a user experience researcher is?

---

12 Megan Campos and Dan Berlin, "Diverse Participant Recruiting Is Essential to Authentic User Research."

13 Dana Chisnell, "Talking to Strangers on the Street: Recruiting Through Intercepting People," *User Experience Magazine* 15, no. 5 (2016).

- Avoid jargon ("personas," "research session," "moderating," and so on) that creates a distance between you and the person you are trying to engage with. You can be professional without jargon.
- Explain what you are doing and why but give them the minimum amount of information. "We're doing some market research with customers" is usually better than "We're developing a series of new features for ChompoDR 9.1 and are looking for feedback to help us prioritize the roadmap."
- Be specific about what you're asking for, with details like:
  - A one-hour conversation
  - At your home
  - In the next two weeks
  - Me and one of my colleagues
  - We'll want to record our conversation.
  - We'll have a release for you to sign ahead of time.
- Be specific about what you're offering, e.g., a $125 gift card.
- Address any concerns you anticipate, e.g., "We don't want to see any of your account details."

Note that the National Center on Disability and Journalism has a "Disability Language Style Guide"[14] for inclusive language that you can use to invite people with disabilities to participate in research.

NOTE BEING VERY SPECIFIC

At one point, I kept finding myself in people's homes for interviews, only to find out at the beginning that the thing I was there to see wasn't actually there. One participant lived apart from the father of her child, and the activity in question took place at the father's house. Another was a flight attendant who met me at his pied-a-terre where none of the artifacts or behavior I wanted to see happened. They qualified for the study, per the screener, but I never specified that the place where we held the interview had to be where those practices were happening. Since then, I make sure that interaction around the invite, scheduling, and confirmation establishes that I'll be able to see whatever it is that I need to see.

---

14 "Disability Language Style Guide," National Center on Disability and Journalism, last revised August 2021.

Recruiting draws heavily on the project management skill set but keep your researcher's eye open for surprises. If it's very challenging to find the people that you expect (or are expected) to do research with, *that's data*. In one project, the fact that I couldn't find anyone with a luxurious, yet functional, "smart home" implementation revealed a great deal about how that client conceived the market.

Scheduling Interviews

If you are interviewing professionals about their work, you may need to run your interviews during (or just before/after) their work hours. If you are interviewing consumers, you may have to conduct interviews in the evening or on weekends. In the latter case, it can be helpful to set that expectation early on with colleagues who will be participating. Remind them that you're trying to embrace the participant's own worldview, and they can begin that process by adapting their schedule and availability to the participant's lifestyle, not the opposite.

When scheduling your fieldwork days, don't be too ambitious. Although focus group and usability moderators tend to set up camp in a facility and run sessions back-to-back for a full day or more, I think that's a terrible idea, especially when doing fieldwork. Quality work doesn't come from being rushed, exhausted, harried, or overwhelmed. Interviewing is hard work. Leave time between sessions, in case they run over, to reflect on what you learned, to debrief your team, to adjust your approach for the next interview, get to the next interview location, find food, find a bathroom, and process anything emotional that comes up. Although this becomes more dramatic when you are driving around a metropolitan area interviewing people in their homes, it's still true when moving around a corporate facility during a site visit or interviewing people remotely from your desk.

Don't pack too many interviews into a day. Depending on the constraints (Are you on-site? Are you on the road? How long are the interviews?), two interviews a day is reasonable. The schedule is at least partly informed by participant availability, so you may end up with an early morning interview, several hours of free time, an evening interview on one day, and then two back-to-back interviews the next day. That's fine. Just don't try to do several days in a row with too many interviews.

For remote interviews, when you're going to be running the session from your desk, beware the downside of remote research: it just looks like another meeting on your calendar. It's extremely difficult to go from, say, a team meeting to an interview, where your orientation and overall mindset needs to shift. Protect your calendar to ensure that you are able to do the interview (including time to prep beforehand, to debrief, write notes, and complete any other post-interview tasks).

Travel

The same sanity clause applies to travel situations. If you're traveling locally, try to schedule your interviews so they are close together geographically. If you're working with recruiters, they should take care of this. If you're traveling on a plane, allow time for your plane to be late before your first interview and avoid having an interview that will run into your head-to-the-airport window, because that will destroy your ability to be present in the interview. Even better, keep travel days and interview days separate. If you are traveling internationally, leave yourself at least a day to adjust to the time zone differences and to soak up the local culture before you dive into fieldwork.

Participant Releases and Nondisclosure Agreements

A *release* is a must. A release is a document that you have your interviewee sign. It clarifies the rights that the interviewee and the interviewer (and their organization) have. The text of the release may address a number of issues, including the following:

- **Consent:** Being in the study is voluntary, and the participant can stop at any time.
- **Incentive:** The amount of money that will be given, and that the exchange of money doesn't mean that the participant is an employee.
- **Model release:** Images and video will be used without giving the participant any rights of approval.
- **Nondisclosure (NDA):** The participant is obligated not to reveal anything about concepts he may see.
- **Data privacy:** It constitutes what data will be collected, how it will be stored, and for how long.

In situations where you are not revealing any concepts of artifacts that might be considered confidential, you may want to streamline the release by eliminating the NDA.

Although there are ethical reasons to use a release, it's really a legal document. Work with your legal department to strike the right balance between legally efficacious terminology and regular-folks lingo (see Figure 2.2).[15]

Don't break stuff. We're happy to have users test our designs and applications. But you may not try to cause harm or damage to our data, systems, or anything else.

Independent contractor. You understand you are not a Company X or Company XY Professionals employee, and are not entitled to related benefits, equity compensation, or any compensation that wasn't clearly described to you in the process of signing up for the Project.

Severability. "Severability" is a fancy way of saying that if a court finds any part of this Agreement invalid, then all the other parts will still be valid.

FIGURE 2.2
Detail from an actual participant release (with the company's identifying information removed). Overall, there's plenty of legalese, but also plenty of friendlier language as well.

While the specifics will vary by the relationship you have with your participant, it's generally better to be clear and specific about rights and expectations. Sometimes it's helpful to send documents ahead of time so that people can review them on their own. If not, it's good to let them know that they will be asked to review and sign a document at the beginning of the session. The alternative—surprising a participant by asking them "Do you mind if we record?" and then having the researcher explain some aspects of what this verbal agreement covers—is not only awkward, but also ethically and legally shaky.[16]

If you work for an agency conducting this research on behalf of a client, the release may be an agreement between your organization and the participant, enabling you to keep the study "blind" (which means the participant does not know the name of the sponsoring organization), which is usually preferable. However, if you work for an agency and your client is asking for nondisclosure, you will probably want to use the client's NDA and have that particular aspect of the agreement be between the participant and the client directly.

---

15 The whole document is at https://portigal.com/release

16 See sections on the agreement ("Informed Consent"), as well as many other aspects of planning user research in Alba Villamil, "The Ethical Researcher's Checklist," June 25, 2020, https://docs.google.com/document/d/1107r9r6d-2-4MwRZX6eiZbMi1LuClOB2sZ88KcQP9ME/edit

Regulations like the European Union's General Data Protection Regulation (GDPR)[17] and the California Consumer Privacy Act (CCPA)[18] set out requirements for companies when collecting and storing data about consumers, as well as the fines or other consequences for failing to follow those requirements. It's important that research activities don't expose the company to legal risks.

At many of the organizations she's worked at, researcher Leanne Waldal has partnered with her legal department to help set up the needed tools and processes. She'll reach out to someone in that team to connect, learn what they do, and talk about what she does. She says, "I need to understand what Legal cares about, so I can include that when I'm making asks."

Sometimes, when describing user research to her legal colleagues, she is met with blank stares. In one situation, Leanne found activities in other parts of the organization (product managers, regularly talking to customers over video, without a signed release, and recording those calls) and used those to persuade her legal team that, in fact, research was happening, whatever it was being called, and those processes and documents were needed.

"Teaching them about user research" can be key to establishing the collaboration. In one organization, she invited her contact (who had been a roadblock) to attend an internal "customer-centricity" class she was teaching; he saw the research process as "fun" and finally understood what it was she was trying to do. Without that explicit lesson, some legal teams may not really grasp the business need that product teams have for showing their app with personal identifiable information (PII).

Leanne compared building a collaboration with her legal department to other challenges that researchers face. For example, researchers have to work to gain access to users when the sales team owns those relationships (see elsewhere in this chapter). They also push to influence decision-makers with the results of research. (See Chapter 10, "Making an Impact with Your Research.") She approaches all of these with the same "bag of tricks."

---

17 Regulation (EU) 2016/679 of the European Parliament and of the Council of 27 April 2016 on the protection of natural persons with regard to the processing of personal data and on the free movement of such data, https://eur-lex.europa.eu/legal-content/EN/TXT/?url=CELEX%3A02016R0679-20160504

18 The California Consumer Privacy Act of 2018, https://oag.ca.gov/privacy/ccpa

Incentives

You should provide an incentive to your user research participants[19] (although this can be a challenging conversation in some startup companies). The right incentive amount depends on where you are doing research and what you are asking of the participant. If you are using a recruiting agency, they can advise you on a recommended incentive.[20] Think of the incentive not as compensation but as an enthusiastically demonstrative thank-you. In professional situations (interviewing people at their workplace), a monetary incentive given directly to the participant may not be appropriate. It may be prohibited by the participant's employer, it may be unethical or at least awkward if your participant is a customer, and if you are interviewing individuals within a group (say an emergency room) on an ad hoc basis, it may be less clear whom to incentivize and at what proportion. In those cases, look for alternatives.

You want a simple and direct way to demonstrate your enthusiasm and appreciation. When interviewing credit-default swap traders in London's financial district, my client escort would stop en route at a Starbucks and load up with Venti drinks and baked goods. Even though we had scheduled appointments, our appearance on the trading floor was a small celebration. We've taken pizza into hospitals when interviewing respiratory techs and made charitable donations to groups supported by employees at our participant's workplace. Some companies offer a discount on their subscription price or early access to products or features. Branded swag can be an option, but make sure it's *something people will value* more than *some free crap sitting in a closet no one wants*; even so, it may be better as a bonus on top of the money than as a substitute. In a business-to-business relationship, the participant organization might appreciate a presentation of what you've learned (keeping in mind the data privacy and other confidentiality concerns you are obligated to respect).

You can use a payment service like Venmo or PayPal, or gift cards, especially if you are dealing with multiple countries. The challenge is to balance the research team's needs (such as efficiency, compliance,

---

19 Sarah Fathallah, "Why Design Researchers Should Compensate Participants," *Medium*, April 7, 2020.

20 Ethnio has an incentive calculator at https://ethn.io/incentives/calculator and User Interviews has one at www.userinterviews.com/lp/ux-research-incentive-calculator

and tax implications) with an easy and positive experience for research participants. At a minimum, make sure that your participants know ahead of time how and when they'll be getting their incentive.

Paying incentives can be an additional part of the service provided by your recruiting agency. For a handling fee, they will mail checks to your participants after interviews are completed (although you should follow up with them to make sure they act promptly).

If you provide a nondigital incentive yourself (as opposed to using a third-party), go beyond a corporate check in a business envelope and include a thank-you note as well.

OPERATIONAL SKILLS FOR RESEARCHERS

By Tamara Hale, Ph.D.

Tamara Hale is a Research, Design and Operations leader with over 17 years' experience. She has built human-first products, services, and teams for Fortune 500 companies, government and nonprofits including Microsoft, Workday, Dropbox, Wells Fargo, and Her Majesty's Revenue and Customs. Tamara was trained as an anthropologist, with a Ph.D. from the London School of Economics and Political Science.

Things are much better today for researchers who are able to partner with Research Ops. If you are lucky to have such a team, give them some love today! Back in the day, I recruited my own users, including physically going out on the rainy streets of London to find people. This was long and tiring work even for an emerging extrovert. To be fair, recruiting agencies existed even back then and have been around for as long as market research has existed, but they were expensive and they couldn't reliably recruit specialized demographics that were often referred to as "hard-to-reach" (anything other than WEIRD—Western, Educated, Industrialized, Rich, and Democratic). In many large enterprise organizations, researchers couldn't directly recruit their own participants and had to work with another team, such as Customer Success, or Sales, or Product. Before Research Ops, it might have taken me between four weeks to four months to recruit users. Once we'd built a Research Ops function, it took two weeks.

continues

While the rise of Research Operations is undoubtedly a good thing, there are a few skills that may have gotten lost along the way in the researcher toolkit. Here are the operational skills the best researchers have:

- **Recruiting:** Your research is only as good as your data and your data is only as good as the quality of your participants. Researchers shouldn't offload key recruiting decisions to Research Ops but need to be active and involved thought partners. One of the biggest gaps I've seen is researchers who have never written a screener or know how the recruiting process works. Every researcher should get hands-on recruiting experience at least once, not least so that they learn how to partner with recruiters.

- **Basic project management:** It's important to create project briefs and plans with clearly defined research objectives that stakeholders are aligned on. (Why? Because stakeholders change their minds, and the worst thing is finishing a study only for your partners to tell you "That's not what we were interested in.") Also, emphasize well-defined roles and responsibilities, cadences for meetings, milestones, and risks and dependencies. (What's out of scope, what are you not addressing, and what are you trading off in the approach are just part of organizing your work and ensuring success down the road.)

- **Research scoping:** You need to know how long it will roughly take you to do a thing. If you don't, you risk overcommitting yourself, or failing to deliver on time, or not even getting the buy-in to start the research. If you've ever had to sell your work directly (as a freelancer or as part of a smaller consulting shop), you probably already have these skills. When research budgets are flowing, these skills are important, but when budgets inevitably tighten, these skills shine.

- **Budgeting:** You will at some point in your career be asking a partner or a leader or a customer for funding. It's essential to have an understanding of what research costs, both time (see above about scoping) and cost-wise.

- **Vendor knowledge:** Great Ops folks have established relationships with a broad range of vendors and are up-to-date on the changing research and software industry and marketplace. They can help match research studies to the right tools, but as a researcher, keeping an open eye on what new products and features are available, or volunteering to use a beta product is a great way to increase your own skills, make the products better for other researchers, and move our field forward.

- **Knowledge management:** Very few Ops teams are fortunate enough to have dedicated research librarians. But if you want your research to be found and used beyond the immediate team or project, then you need to have an awareness of and appreciation for consistent archiving and organization of research data. It also helps the researchers who come after you.

- **Socialization and communications:** Your research isn't done when you deliver the report. Finding repeatable, recognizable ways to turn your research into an artifact or product that can be accessed and expected by different stakeholders and being creative with your media while targeting different audiences extends the life and impact of your research.

- **Process improvement overall:** Research Ops works best when it's in close collaboration with research. Researchers don't get to offload process improvements to Ops. They should try things out and then partner with Ops to improve and scale to whole teams. Research is a team effort, so is Operations.

There's still a long way to go in terms of organizations recognizing the true value of Research Operations. Ultimately, the mission of Ops is to make research not just faster and more efficient, but better, more ethical, more sustainable, and more impactful to the business.

The Interview Guide

The interview guide (sometimes called a *field guide* or *discussion guide* or more formally, a *protocol*) is a document that details what will happen in the interview (see Figure 2.3).[21] Creating this detailed plan is an essential preparatory step. The interviews themselves almost never happen as you imagine, but having a detailed plan prepares you to be flexible. It also creates alignment among the team (as do other planning tools). In situations where you have multiple teams of people out in the field, this alignment is essential.

FIGURE 2.3

An excerpt of an interview guide shows a hypothetical flow of how the interview could proceed.

Reading Ahead Interview Guide

Introduction (5 min)

- Give out release form and get signature
- Turn on video camera
- Confirm timing
- Who are we and why are we doing this
- There no wrong answers, this is information that help us direct our work

1. We'd like to talk with you today about reading. We have lots of questions to ask you, and we're interested in hearing your stories and experiences.

Overview (10 min)

2. Can you tell us a little about yourself—what you do, hobbies, etc.?

3. Can you tell me about a recent book you've read? Your favorite all-time book?

4. Why do you read?

5. What is your current reading like?

[Probe for different types of reading, locations, motivations, etc.]

6. Is your current reading typical for you? How so/how is it different?

7. Do you call yourself a "reader?" What does that mean to you?

[Look for their categories: could be frequency, importance, etc.]

If you were telling a new acquaintance about yourself, would you talk about reading? What else would you say about yourself?

Exploring Specifics (locations, subject matter, motivations) (10 min)

8. You mentioned (follow up on specifics from overview). Is this always the same, or does it change? Why do you do it this way?

9. Have there been any special circumstances where you've done it differently? Why? How was that?

10. Has anything about the way you do this changed over time? How? Why?

Environment (5 min)

11. What makes a good reading environment for you? What are the elements? What makes an environment not good?

To prepare your interview guide, start with your research goals and the other inputs. This is the step, as mentioned in Chapter 1, "Interviewing Addresses a Business Need," where you translate research questions into participant questions. Of course, the guide also covers activities, tasks, logistics, and more.

---

21 The complete example is at https://portigal.com/interview-guide

The general flow of most interview guides is:

- Introduction and participant background
- The main body
- Projection/dream questions
- Wrap up

Be sure to assign durations to the different sections and subsections. Again, you aren't necessarily going to stick to the exact duration in the actual interview, but it helps you see if you've got enough time to cover everything you are expecting to cover. I prefer to write most questions as I might ask them ("Is there a single word that captures the thing you most like about wine?"), rather than as abstract topics ("A single word that represents what they like about wine?"). As I'm writing the interview guide, I'm leading a mock interview in my head. Using more detailed, thought-out questions helps me put together a more realistic plan.

Introduction and Participant Background

In the introduction, you'll spend just a few minutes getting the interview underway, handling some logistics, and setting expectations. This section of the interview guide might contain the following:

- Give out release forms and get signatures.
- Turn on video camera.
- Confirm timing.
- Explain who you are and why you are doing this.
- There are no wrong answers; this is information that helps you direct your work.
- Tell us about your family. Who lives in this house? How long have you lived here?

For now, you're just writing the interview guide, but in Chapter 4, "The Successful Fieldwork Experience," you'll learn more about using the logistics of kicking off the interview.

The Main Body

As the name suggests, this is the bulk of the interview guide (and the interview). You should create subsections for each of the areas you want to explore (such as configuration, learning about features, downloading new playlists). The main body should also include the exercises and activities that you plan to use (such as mapping, card sorting, demonstrations, and reactions to prototypes or other stimuli).

For a study seeking feedback about a prototype home entertainment device, our main body topics were:

- Revisit concepts
- Map your technology
- Context of use
- Concept discussion

Be deliberate in how you sequence these sections. You can start with the general and then dive into specifics; you can start with present day and move backward; you can start with a previous time and move toward the current state. There's no universal rule here, so much depends on your topic and how you are mentally picturing the inquiry. Remember the participant may take things in a different direction, so don't sweat too much over this. It's easy to revise the overall flow once you've completed a couple of the interviews.

Projection/Dream Questions

Near the end of the interview is a great opportunity to ask more audacious questions. Because you've spent all this time with your participants, talking through a topic in detail, they've become engaged with you. You've earned their permission to ask them to go even farther beyond the familiar. Questions that work really well here are:

- If we came back in five years to have this conversation again, what would be different?
- If you could create your ideal experience, what would it be like?
- If you had a magic wand, what would you change about this experience?

Wrap Up

A typical interview guide concludes with some basic questions and instructions:

- Did we miss anything? Is there anything you want to tell us? Or that you think we should know?
- Is there anything you want to ask us?
- Thank them and give the incentive.

Shot List

As an appendix to the interview guide, list the photos you want to capture (see Figure 2.4), such as the following:

- Head shot of participant
- Participant and key piece of equipment
- Close-up of key piece of equipment
- Action shot of participant using equipment (e.g., doing the activity you're studying)
- Establishing shots, interior (cubicle or living room) and exterior
- Two-shot of interviewer and participant
- Action shot of researchers/clients/stakeholders "doing research"

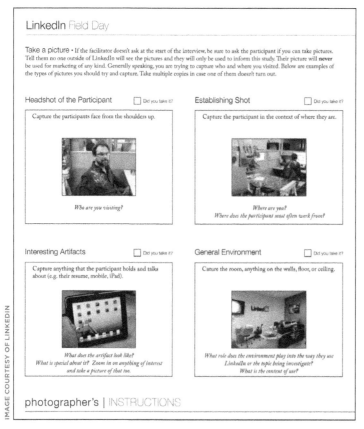

FIGURE 2.4

A shot list created from LinkedIn provides researchers with a visual reminder of what images to capture during the interview.

Socialize the Guide

As with the other preparation tools, share the interview guide with your team. The typical audience for the interview guide tends to be broader than for the more tactical tools like a screener. I also try to help the people reviewing it understand what the interview guide is (and what it isn't) so that they can effectively help it evolve. I've used the following in an explanatory email:

> Remember, this is not a script. It reads very linearly, but it's really just a tool to prepare to be flexible. Questions don't get asked in the order they're written here or using this exact language (so it doesn't need to be proofread). If you could look at it with an eye toward calling out anything that we haven't covered—e.g., "We need to ask about how they deal with time zones"—or any larger topic areas that are missing, or anything that seems wildly off base, that would be the most helpful.

NOTE A MODULAR INTERVIEW GUIDE

Michael Davis Burchat created a modular interview guide with questions on individual cards that he could spread out on the table between him and the participant (see Figure 2.5). He found that this helped build rapport by reducing the sense of distance between the two people, making it a more collaborative and transparent exchange.

FIGURE 2.5
A modular interview guide helps shift to a more collaborative dynamic between participant and interviewer.

The Last Word

It takes a lot of preparation—perhaps a surprising amount—to set up successful field research. I don't recommend leaping into the fieldwork without setting yourself up to be successful. The effort in creating alignment, developing a plan, and determining the logistics pays off tremendously in the quality of the experience for you, your stakeholders, and your participants, as well as in the value of the insights gathered.

- Agreeing to the objectives for field research is crucial but is often challenging. You may all agree that you are going to interview 12 typical users before you are able to agree on what you expect to learn and how that will inform your business.

- Use the documents you create in planning (research goals, screener, and interview guide) to align with your team.

- Consider broadly and choose specifically what types of participants you want. But treat this as a hypothesis and adjust your approach, if necessary.

- Leave time in your project plan to find research participants.

- The interview guide is the detailed plan of what you *think* might happen in the interview, typically flowing from the details to their meaning. Having that detailed plan empowers you to be flexible when you actually go into the field.

- When scheduling interviews, leave adequate time between them for reflection, eating, travel, and the bathroom. Don't overload your day—and your poor brain—with too many interviews.

- Use a release form that documents the rights and obligations of both the organization that sponsors the research and the participant.

- Give participants an incentive that conveys your sincere appreciation of their time.

CHAPTER 3

Contextual Methods—More Than Just Asking Questions

Although the title of this book emphasizes *interviewing*, when you get down to it, *interviewing* involves more than just *interviewing*. Wow. Okay. Phew. Now, let's move on! Interviewing is absolutely the core of the interaction with your participant, but interviewing supports other techniques as well (or if you prefer, *methods*). You should consider the interview itself as a platform and try to integrate a larger set of techniques organically.

> **NOTE** SAY THE RIGHT THING
>
> Sam Ladner taught me to stop using the word "methodology" when I mean "method." As she explained *"Method* is to *methodology* as *zoo* is to *zoology*. Methods are the things you actually do, just like the zoo is a place you actually visit. Methodology and zoology are the study of those things." For example, *interviewing* is a method, but *phenomenology* is a methodology. I always mean "method."

Prework

Often, the thing we are most interested in happens in a series of smaller interactions over a course of days and weeks. In that case, give your participant a homework assignment. For example, when I wanted to understand how people would react to a credit card newsletter, I asked participants to save their postal mail for a few days, without opening it. During our interview, they went through this pile of mail and narrated their sorting process, explaining what they would keep and what they would discard. When I then showed our prototype newsletter in its envelope, we had a solid context for investigating their expectations for the newsletter. Similarly, when Beringer was redesigning its Stone Cellars wine packaging, we asked our participants to save a week's worth of empty bottles. Between their unopened wine, the empty bottles, and the sample bottles we brought with us, we had a wide range of example packages to look at together.

I also use homework as a way to *prime* participants about a topic I'm interested in. In other words, this activity helps people reach a state where they are more introspective about an aspect of their behavior that they might not pay attention to otherwise. I've asked people to log when they use their mobile phone, take screenshots of every intranet search, or document all their banking activities. And while this activity produces provocative and intriguing examples, as well as weak signals about possible behavior patterns, the real value of this self-documentation (sometimes called *journaling* or a *diary study*) really pays off during a follow-up interview. Not only do you have an extensive set of examples to discuss, but you also have a participant who has been thinking about a topic a lot more than they normally would have. (You can see this happen during interviews as well; I'll discuss this more in Chapter 4, "The Successful Fieldwork Experience.") Of course, if your goal is to understand what's already top of mind, don't prime your participant.

You can also use priming to accelerate the usage of a product. I brought a networked music device to the homes of digital music enthusiasts and asked them to install it while I watched. At the end of the interview, I left them with a workbook that contained about two weeks' worth of assignments, asking them to explore a different feature or use case. Given that people would be unlikely to explore a product that thoroughly in two weeks (if ever, especially given the complexity of this particular product), it was crucial to give people a structure—and a motivation—to drive their usage. After two weeks, we collected their workbooks and then returned for a follow-up interview.

A third form of prework prompts users for anecdotes, stories, or examples of the themes you're most interested in. This could be a survey with a few open-ended questions, or you might ask people to submit a photo with a brief explanation. Ask for both successful and unsuccessful examples.

For a study about how people organized their financial information, we asked people to email us two photographs.

1. An example of something you keep organized the way you'd like it to be. It could be information, physical items, digital items, or whatever.

2. An example of something that you have outsourced to someone else. You aren't responsible for dealing with this thing any longer and have some comfort in knowing it's being taken care of by someone else.

In another study, about remote work, we used an online form and asked people the following questions:

1. Can you provide a recent example when you were **successful with a sustained focus** on your work? What was the situation? What was it that enabled you to sustain that focus?

2. Can you provide a recent example when you were **challenged in trying to focus** on your work? What was the situation? What were the reasons this was challenging?

In both cases, we started the interview by acknowledging their examples and asking them to tell us about the stories in more detail.

NOTE THE DOG ATE THEIR HOMEWORK

Assigning prework can reveal recruited participants who are too busy or not fully engaged. If they don't respond, or respond late, or respond without much detail or insight, you can prioritize other participants for follow-up interviews.

Showing and Telling

Even when your only technique is asking questions, there are many ways to get to the information you are seeking. I'll go further into the types of questions in Chapter 6, "The Intricacies of Asking Questions." The phrasing of the question itself leads to a variety of techniques. If one of your research objectives is to understand how people are managing their digital music, you might ask your participants specifically, "What is your process for updating your playlists?" With that question, the participant is being asked to verbally summarize a (potentially detailed) behavior from memory. This isn't necessarily a bad approach; it may be interesting to hear which steps in the process are memorable and which ones aren't.

It's also a chance to get some emotional color. ("Oh, it's easy, all I do is....") But it's not going to be the most accurate information. By asking, "What is your process for updating your playlists?" you are actually learning the answers to the (unasked) "How do you feel about the process for updating playlists?" and "What are the key steps you can recall in the process for updating playlists?" That information is very important, but it may not be sufficient to really understand the user's situation.

Now, a slightly different expression of the question is "Can you show me how you update your playlists?" Now you've staged an activity. In this activity, you and your participant will move to where the relevant devices are, and you will be able to observe the specific steps in completing this task. Of course, you're also going to gather the emotional context of the process. I sat with a financial advisor who struggled to navigate his intranet in order to find some critical data. His lack of success in locating this data was so frustrating that he began to laugh. Of course, it wasn't comical per se, but he felt that the failures of the system were absolutely ludicrous, and the laughter clearly revealed his perspective.

Although a topic such as playlist updating may be specific to that participant's personal devices and data, in situations where the process is more general, you may try a slight variation, shifting to a participant-observation dialogue, such as, "Can you show me how I should prepare coffee?" Instead of the subject going through their own process, narrating the different steps as *they* would perform them, your question directs them to explain specifically each step so that *you* can perform it, such as, "Now, before you put the filter in, make sure the water is boiling." Asking that person to play the teacher role not only reinforces the idea that they are the expert here, but it can also make it easier for them to articulate the details you are seeking.

Depending on the activity, you may arrange to be present when it occurs. I once sat in a family's kitchen at 7:00 a.m. and watched as they went through their morning food prep rituals. (Yes, that was very early. The only thing worse than the feeling of getting up so early to do fieldwork was the look on the participants' faces when they opened the door to let me in. Sure, they agreed to it ahead of time, but I was certainly not their favorite person at that particular moment.) I didn't need to ask them to show me how coffee was prepared because I knew ahead of time that this was when coffee was going to be prepared. In addition to seeing the operation of the coffee machine, I saw a great deal of context—what other devices were being used, who else was around, what happened before, and what happened after.

You can also work with your participant to stage the activity you want to understand. Although you can expect that breakfast will be eaten most days, you can't be sure that the IT department will be installing a new router every day. However, if you bring them a router when you come for your interview, you've created the occasion.

Another approach more suited for unpacking interactions between people is role-playing how this interaction does (or should) take place. In a project where we looked at customer service experiences, a man complained emphatically but without specificity about the phone service at his local department store. I asked him what he objected to, or how it could be different, but he struggled to find anything to tell me beyond his general dissatisfaction with the way things were. Instead, I suggested that he act as the person answering the phone, and I would act as him, and he could show me how it should work. After describing the exercise, I held an imaginary phone to my head and said "Ring, ring!" (See Figure 3.1.) He answered his imaginary phone, and we proceeded to model the ideal conversation. Afterward, we talked about how our version differed from his typical experience.

FIGURE 3.1
Shifting the discussion from the conceptual to the tangible (even when being tangible means being fantastical) is one way to get at hard-to-uncover information.

No one of the interrelated techniques in this chapter is inherently better than the others. Any of them may be appropriate, depending on what you want to know, what you've already asked, and what is working well between you and your participant. You may also want to combine these approaches to look for points of divergence. For example, if you observe a certain coffee preparation step that is excluded from the process your participant teaches you, that's something you can ask about: "I noticed that when you were making coffee earlier you waited until the water boiled before you put the filter in. That wasn't something you told me to do. Is it an important part of the process?" As with so many aspects of the work you're doing, you want to have a broad palette of approaches that you can bring to bear as circumstances warrant.

Bring the Tools

When you conduct research on-site, you get to observe the details of your user's environment. But you also have the opportunity to bring items into that environment. There are several techniques that involve using prepared physical materials to facilitate the interview, including maps, various forms of representing concepts, organizing and sorting artifacts, and "provocative" images.

Mapping

A map is a tangible representation that shifts the abstract (such as a process, a set of relationships, or the details of a large physical space) into a concrete artifact. This artifact provides a focal point for more detailed discussions, and the documentation can be taken with you at the end of the interview. In one project, we asked architects and designers to map out their fairly complex workflow (indicating software packages, file formats, processes, contributors, output, and so on) using sticky notes (where each color represented a certain class of element) on a large piece of butcher paper. Tom Williams of Point Forward has used actual city maps to have people show him the details of their lives, asking them to draw on the map specifics such as their route to get to work, their favorite coffee shop, where they like to go for walks, and so on.

In a project for Nokia Research Center that explored opportunities emerging from the convergence of entertainment devices and home computing, tech-savvy consumers drew a map of their homes and indicated where their technology was located and how it was connected together (see Figure 3.2). The interviewer facilitated the process of drawing the map by probing and prompting. As the map was built, both the participant and the interviewer developed a shared understanding. As the interview proceeded, the interviewer could continually refer to the information on the map—for example, by pointing to an element and clarifying "So that would be when you're over here, then?" The map became a crucial element in the analysis and synthesis work after the fieldwork was over, as the interviewer used it to relate pertinent details to his colleagues.

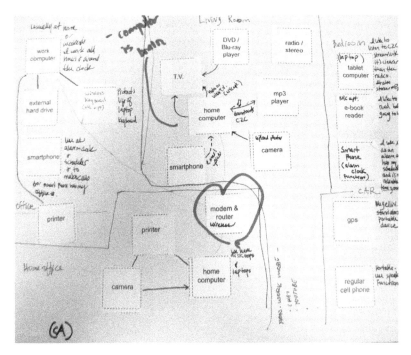

FIGURE 3.2

A participant's hand-drawn map shows how technology was connected together in their home.

Other Exercises

Exercises are a way to provide some structure to your enquiry. You might ask someone to draw a timeline, prioritize a set of items, write a love letter/breakup letter for a product they use/want to stop using, write alternative slogans for advertising images of your product, do a word association for each of your product attributes, and so on. You can legitimize these exercises by designing a worksheet to take with you, along with different types of pens, markers, and stickers. It should be simple and potentially fun (depending on the topic), but making a worksheet adds formality, and it gives the participant something they can work on independently during the interview.

Participatory Design

Participatory design, which sometimes refers to an overall approach to design, is essentially giving people the tools to show them how they can envision a new design or solution. It can take many forms.

For example, I've created blank versions of a mobile device screen and had participants draw the UI, and I've seized the moment when participants started envisioning a new solution and helped them grab whatever was nearby. (One participant grabbed a hard cover book as a proxy for a size-and-form factor, but then proceeded to gesture with the book as if it really were this future device.)

Designers sometimes get nervous with participatory design because it implies that users will tell them what to design, and they'll be expected to go off and implement it. Of course, that's not true at all. Participants may decide their ideal product needs a handle. But we know that really means that they need an easy way to move it from place to place, and we know that there are dozens of ways to satisfy that need. My aim with participatory design is to give people a different way to talk about needs, where the solutions stand as proxies for those needs.

Reactions to Concepts

In some situations, you'll want to get feedback on a specific solution. But in other situations, your objective is more about deeply understanding the problem space or opportunities for new solutions. What you present need not represent an actual solution. Rather than repurposing the visual artifacts that are part of your team's design process, create some new stimuli just for research. Show concepts that are not viable or otherwise unlikely in order to explore the edges of factors that influence desirability, usefulness, and so on (see Figure 3.3). What you're learning is not an evaluation of the concept (e.g., "concept testing"), but instead a deeper understanding of the design criteria for a future solution. Although concepts are the stimuli, you deliberately choose stimuli that contain some aspect of your hypotheses, ideas, or questions in a tangible form.

As with participatory design, solutions that you show can stand as proxies for something else. You aren't asking questions about their *needs* (say, their expectations for a device's size), but rather you are asking questions about a *concept* in order to elicit, among other feedback, their expectations for the device's size. This can be quite indirect; the stimuli don't actually reveal to the participant what it is that you want to know, what is feasible, what is planned, or what your hypotheses are. There's a difference between what you want to know and what you ask. Let yourself be creative when developing these provocative stimuli.

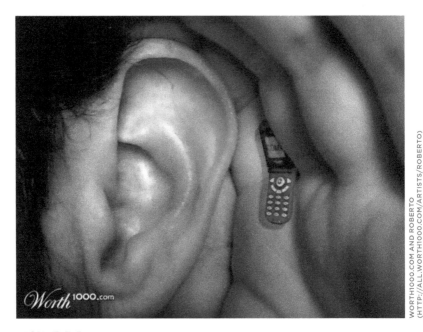

FIGURE 3.3
Although you wouldn't develop a mobile phone this tiny, you could provoke an interesting dialogue by showing it to someone. It would be much harder to have a discussion about button size, screen size, ear-canal risk, and so on, if you only had a set of "best" solutions on hand.

You should go to the interview with a set of specific aspects of the stimuli that you're looking for feedback about, but it's important to let the participants structure most of the responses themselves. Put the concept in front of them, with whatever explanation or demonstration, and then stop talking. If absolutely necessary, try an open-ended question such as "What do you think?" The topics they choose themselves are the strongest natural reactions. If they start off raving about the keyboard but don't mention the screen until you ask about it, that's an important takeaway. It's your job to make sure that you hear about the keyboard, the screen, and all the other topics of interest, but the concerns and delights that they express unprompted are critical.

It's usually appropriate to do a short interview first, to get some basic context about how they currently behave and how they might imagine things being different in the future. When you hear their preferences or expectations based on your stimuli, it will be easier to understand why they have those preferences, which is ultimately more valuable information.

One caution here: depending on your individual role, you may feel a certain amount of ownership of the concept. But as you'll learn in Chapter 5, "Best Practices for Interviewing," you should check your worldview at the door and be ready to embrace how someone else sees the world. You should present your concepts neutrally in order to give the participants as much freedom in their responses as possible. Avoid "This is something I've been working on," or "I'm really excited to show you this prototype" where mentioning yourself inadvertently pressures your participant to respond positively.

Before you go into the field, practice "the reveal" aloud until you hear yourself sounding neutral. Try "Here's a whole bunch of early ideas that I was asked to show you," or "I'll be curious to hear what you think of this one," or "Our clients are exploring some possible ideas." Here you are distancing yourself from any ownership of the ideas and limiting that associated pressure. In some cases, the concepts themselves are sufficiently complex (because of the technology that's being used or the domain of work that is being supported) that it may be challenging for you to present them effectively. When that happens, partner with someone who is closer to the details or technology to handle that part of the interview: You will introduce the exercise (with neutral language), your colleague will give a neutral demonstration of the concept, and you'll handle the follow-up.

One more caution here: If participants perceive you as having ownership over the concept, they may turn the interview back on you: "Will this be backward-compatible?" "How much will it cost?" "Does it have high fructose corn syrup in the sauce?" *Do not answer those questions.* Once you step into that role and become the expert, it's very hard to backtrack to bland curiosity about their preferences and expectations. This is a terrible struggle for my clients who always have the answers and would feel so much more comfortable in the familiar scenario where they are the experts about this topic. When this happens, do the *Interviewer Sidestep* and turn the question back to them: "Is that important to you?" "What would you expect it to be?" If that feels too confrontational, you can go slightly meta, "I'm going to give you the 'researcher's response,' and ask you 'Is that important to you?'"

IMPROVISING WITH A WOUNDED PROTOTYPE

Working with Hewlett-Packard on research for their DVD/digital projector, I met up with my client at the Denver airport a few hours before we were to head out for our first interview. He was traveling with an *engineering breadboard*, which is a working model cobbled together from parts and controls and stuffed into an electronics case. (This is a "works like" but not a "looks like.") Too big to carry on, it came as checked baggage. Oops.

While it was physically intact, my client quickly realized that the audio no longer worked. In our scant time, we scrambled to borrow multitools and other weapons of engineering destruction. The back seat of our rental car became a mobile bench as he struggled in vain to repair it before fieldwork commenced. In the end, it was fine, even without sound. We showed participants how the device played a DVD and projected the image on their walls. And then we asked them to describe the qualities of the audio they would expect in order to match the video experience the prototype delivered. For more about this project, see **https://portigal.com/hp-case-study**. ■

Reactions to Other Stuff

Other stimuli can be helpful in probing people's underlying belief structures, expectations, or motivations. As with the mapping tools, these stimuli are an interactive and tangible way to help people express themselves. And as before, there are endless ways to provoke participants. Here are just a couple.

Images That Resonate

These images can also be cards, a printed sheet, or stickers (see Figure 3.4). Whatever the medium, they depict a large number of images that are meant to evoke an emotional reaction. Consider stock photos, glamour shots of products, celebrities, historical images, nature and landscape images, textures, colors, and so on. (A variation might be to include words in the set as well.) With this large set of diverse stimuli, you can ask people to pick a few images that address something you're interested in.

In past projects, I've asked people to select images that evoked their ideal online experience with our client's brand, or that represented the way they hoped a new printer could change their lives. The most insightful part happens when you ask participants why they picked those images. They'll tell you—in surprising ways—what it is about those images that speaks to them and how those characteristics represent their hopes, aspirations, or ideal solution.

FIGURE 3.4
Laminated image cards are used to provoke individual reactions and uncover hidden associations.

Casual Card Sort

In contrast to the more rigorous card-sorting process that is used in software design,[1] this is a way to prompt a discussion about a large set of items. For one project, I used cards that depicted a large set of online services (see Figure 3.5). For another project, the cards illustrated many items that people purchased on a regular basis. As the cards were spread out, people began to talk about those that were relevant to them, prompting stories or highlighting areas for follow-up questions. Some groupings may emerge with this process, and the cards can be used as a tool for confirming your understanding of the participant's mental model, as in "So it sounds like these two cards would go together because you see these as examples of something you do for work, but not for your personal use?" Of course, you can create new cards based on what you hear (bring blank ones!), or you can annotate the cards to reflect what the participant has told you.

---

1   You can find a great primer on traditional card sorting at
    https://boxesandarrows.com/card-sorting-a-definitive-guide/

Researchers also use cards with printed phrases on them. In one study, I simply brought small stickies with me, and as I spoke with my participant, I wrote down the key items and phrases on notes and arranged them in front of them. Then we shifted to talking about the set of stickies and how we might refine and organize them.

In this case, I did the writing as a way of giving them space just to talk and signaling that I was listening by handling the documentation myself. Alternatively, you can ask your participant to do the writing themselves, placing the pen and stickies (or whatever you are using) right in front of them. Some people are more or less comfortable in this role, so pay attention and adjust your approach accordingly.

FIGURE 3.5
The primary online services that our research participant mentioned were selected from a larger set.

Concept Formats

There is no limit to the manner of concepts you can develop for researching with users. But it's important to realize that you are creating these concepts for that very purpose: showing to users. You've probably seen shiny prototypes that were intended to get investors, retailers, or managers excited. But I urge clients to represent their ideas in lower, rather than higher, fidelity.[2] As a rule of thumb, lower-fidelity prototypes are best for getting reactions earlier in the process (when you are trying to understand the appeal of the idea), and higher-fidelity prototypes are better for later in the process (when you want to verify some specific aspect of the implementation). There

---

2   For an engaging and helpful read, see Stephanie Houde and Charles Hill, "What Do Prototypes Prototype?" in *Handbook of Human-Computer Interaction* (Second Edition), ed. Martin G. Helander, Thomas K. Landauer, and Prasad V. Prabhu (Amsterdam: Elsevier, 1997), 367–381.

are always exceptions. If you are presenting a futuristic concept, you may want to be very high fidelity in your representation in order to get participants past the inevitable "Well, what would that actually be like?" questions and into the area you want to explore.

High fidelity is not an all-encompassing term. There are different dimensions of fidelity—for example, "looks like" versus "works like." A prototype that simulates an experience may be high fidelity along one dimension but not another.

Be prepared to make something just for conducting research. It's okay for that thing to be less polished than the current state of your design work. Don't simply repurpose the assets from the design process simply because they are available. Ensure that the stimulus artifacts represent your concept in a way that that will be the most effective for your research question.

Here are a few formats for presenting concepts:

- **Storyboard:** An illustration, typically across multiple panels, depicting a scenario. I used storyboards (see Figure 3.6) when working with MediaMaster, a digital music startup that was trying to choose among a number of different directions in their product development.

Step 2
At checkout, Associate scans barcode on front of envelope. Upon purchase, envelope is "activated".

Step 3
When Megan gets home, she follows directions on the envelope and takes the CD booklets out of her CD cases. She counts the booklets, puts them in the envelope.

Step 4
Megan goes online to complete the purchase, selects file formats, and signs-up for a free account. She then drops the envelope in the mail.

FIGURE 3.6
Here is a detail of one of several storyboards showing the different scenarios that MediaMaster was considering developing. Since the research question was about the concept, the images show the usage but not the specifics of the design itself.

- **Physical mock-up:** A representation of a physical product that can be touched, opened, and so on. The team at Nokia Research Center mocked up a number of size variations on a mobile device using foam core and a printout of a screen design (see Figure 3.7, left). Tursiogear, a startup company, provided an early manufacturing prototype of an iPod video case that I showed to consumers in order to help understand the features they were expecting (see Figure 3.7, right).

FIGURE 3.7

Physical mock-ups from Nokia (left) and Tursiogear (right) help make the conversation about a future product tangible.

I've even used this physical mock-up approach for nontechnology projects. When studying how people reacted to different messages in a gas company's credit card newsletter, I used fairly realistic examples of this newsletter, complete with a sample credit card statement and their official envelope. Although most of the newsletter was actual English, the back page had a number of articles with "Greeked" text (lorem ipsum, and so on). One participant noticed this text and (thinking that it was Spanish) commented that the inclusion of a second language was a great idea! It was a good reminder that our assumptions about elements in a concept are often shattered in the field.

In a slightly more challenging situation, I arrived at the research session to find that my client, who was not Apple, had echoed (to put it charitably) the iPhone form factor in a solid model mock-up for a hand-held device. (Their logic was that they were going to try to mock it up later using an iPhone, so....) Every participant therefore assumed that the product would be made by Apple (it wasn't), and that it would be usable not only around the home but also could be taken out and used away from the home (it wouldn't). I had to adjust for those influencing factors in interpreting the results of the sessions.

- **Wireframe:** A simplified version of an on-screen interface. This could be printed, sketched on paper, or a combination. It could be presented on a screen (say, a laptop or tablet). It could be a series of screens that depict a flow with real or simulated interactivity. We showed currency traders a data-free mock-up of their trading platform to uncover which elements had to be carried forward into a redesign and which elements they were receptive to seeing changed. In the previously mentioned Nokia Research Center project, their team produced an iPad-based simulation of a mobile device UI (see Figure 3.8) that we used in combination with a physical mock-up (see Figure 3.7, left).

FIGURE 3.8
Nokia used an iPad to demonstrate the on-screen interaction for a future product concept.

Observation and Shadowing

While interviews are about a verbal interaction with a participant, there are situations where you want to see how people are going about their tasks but are unable to—or choose not to—interact with them directly.

Observation focuses on how people use a physical (or virtual/digital) environment over a period of time. This might consist of all the activity in a restaurant kitchen, how a mobile blood donation van works, or a new car owner getting an insurance quote online.

Shadowing follows an individual or group through activities and locations, like a dog walker from pickup through walking through drop-off, a politician's day of campaigning, or a medical office receptionist from opening through the morning rush.

Both methods emphasize paying attention to what's happening without asking questions. Whether or not you can ask questions depends on how you've arranged to do either observation or shadowing. Shadowing participants have agreed to have you there and may offer their own reflections and narrations or take breaks from their process to answer questions. Observation participants are usually doing their normal thing, unaware that research is taking place.

Still, the questions that you want to ask can be a significant outcome of these methods. Indeed, you might arrange for an interview before or after the period of time to ask about what you expect to see or what you actually saw.

These methods can be challenging because you are exposed to a lot of information but none of it seems meaningful. It feels like "So what, they're just shopping!" "They're just sitting!" There are several frameworks that help you focus and capture what's important. These frameworks list categories to note what you are seeing. Two classic frameworks are POEMS[3] (which stands for People, Objects, Environments, Messages, Services) and AEIOU[4] (Activities, Environments, Interactions, Objects, Users). Make a worksheet[5] with either set of terms as headers and document what you observe accordingly.

You can also adapt this approach into an observation guide[6] with prompts for what you should pay attention to. Here's a basic structure you can adapt.

---

3 Vijay Kumar and Patrick Whitney, "Faster, Cheaper, Deeper User Research," *Design Management Journal* (Spring 2003): 50–57.

4 Christina Wasson, "Ethnography in the Field of Design," *Human Organization* 59, no. 4 (2000): 377–388.

5 Sample worksheets at https://portigal.com/observation-frameworks

6 Download this guide at https://portigal.com/observation-guide

Observation Guide

Observe

- What do they do first? Next?

  Interactions/People

  - Who do they interact with? Include eye contact, gestural, verbal.
  - How long? What is their effect? What do you sense about the people and their interactions?
  - What are the roles people are taking?

  Objects

  - What are they carrying?
  - What do they use? Technology or other?
  - What do they make use of that's already in the environment?
  - What seems to be working well, what seems to be challenging?

  Environment

  - How do they use the environment? Where within the space do they go? Where do they not go?
  - When do they leave? What do you think they would do next?

NOTE EXERCISE: SUSPEND YOUR SENSES

Try this exercise to develop your observation skills. Find somewhere safe but active where you can sit or stand with your eyes closed. For a few minutes, reflect on what you are observing, even if you can't actually see it. Next, find a location where you can observe people interacting with each other, at a distance. Spend a few minutes just watching people and seeing what inferences or assumptions you generate. In both activities you are observing the environment without one of your primary senses,[7] but you're also reflecting on how you observe.

---

7 Of course, people with significant hearing or sight impairments do a version of this exercise every day.

In user research, you're typically observing people within their culture. Culture here is the unspoken rules around behavior that a group has in common. Obvious examples of groups with a particular culture include geographic (people who live in the outskirts of Tulsa, people who live in Hong Kong), but there are also shared cultural characteristics in skateboarders, employees at Mango-Tech's shipping hub, genealogy enthusiasts, and recently graduated radiology technicians. Pay attention to what's "normal" in that culture, especially if it's something that challenges what's normal in your culture. A sign on an office fridge that says "Your mother doesn't work here," or teenagers fixing their hair on the metro, or an advertisement featuring an unfamiliar spokesperson can all be clues about what people value and how and why they do what they do.

Even More Methods

This isn't an exhaustive list of research methods, and you should feel free to combine, tweak, and even make up new methods entirely. Sometimes it's in the moment, like the example earlier in this chapter when I role-played a phone call in the middle of an interview.

Sometimes it's more intentional, like the group activity I designed for a client who wanted to understand some of the expectations people would have for technology that knew a great deal about them and adapted its performance based on that knowledge. We were dealing with a topic that was futuristic in nature, although where it did exist, it was mostly invisible (like a website that loads its home page in the assumed language based on knowing where you are physically located). So, we organized a session where participants were asked to imagine they were either the inhabitants of a "smart home," or the actual elements of the smart home (e.g., kitchen, bathroom, garage). To keep things loose, we had participants wear silly signs indicating their role (see Figure 3.9). We asked them to act out a scenario (say, the family came home from going to a movie) and then ran a debrief session about the scene, analyzing what was successful or unsuccessful and what the underlying design principles were. It was fun, and effective, but the point here is that I made this up.[8] You can make up methods, too!

---

8   This method shares some DNA with Informance (see Colin Burns, Eric Dishman, William Verplank, and Bud Lassiter, "Actors, Hairdos & Video-tape—Informance Design," *CHI '94 Conference Companion on Human Factors in Computing Systems*, 1994, 119–120.

Hello, my name is Bathroom.

FIGURE 3.9
Participants in the
"smart home" activity
wore fanciful signs
indicating their role in
the scenario.

The Last Word

Be creative in developing a range of methods for any one project. While interviewing is at the core, it's really a platform that can support other techniques that go beyond merely asking questions. You can vary the activities in the session itself, ask participants to prepare for the interview, or bring materials specifically to facilitate the discussion.

- Ask for a demonstration of an activity that might not otherwise take place.

- Observe a behavior or a task as it happens to occur naturally.

- Use a mapping exercise to create a tangible representation of something abstract that you can refer to repeatedly throughout the interview (and then take away with you at the end).

- Show provocative concepts at varying levels of fidelity and create concepts that will generate discussion around the issues at hand (rather than testing your best guess at the best solution).

- Use images as stimuli to prompt a deeper discussion; when mounted on cards, they can be sorted, grouped, annotated, referred to later, and so on.

- Assign homework (for example, take a few pictures, save some artifacts, complete a questionnaire, and document a set of activities) to give you some data before the interview and to prime the participant about the interview topics.

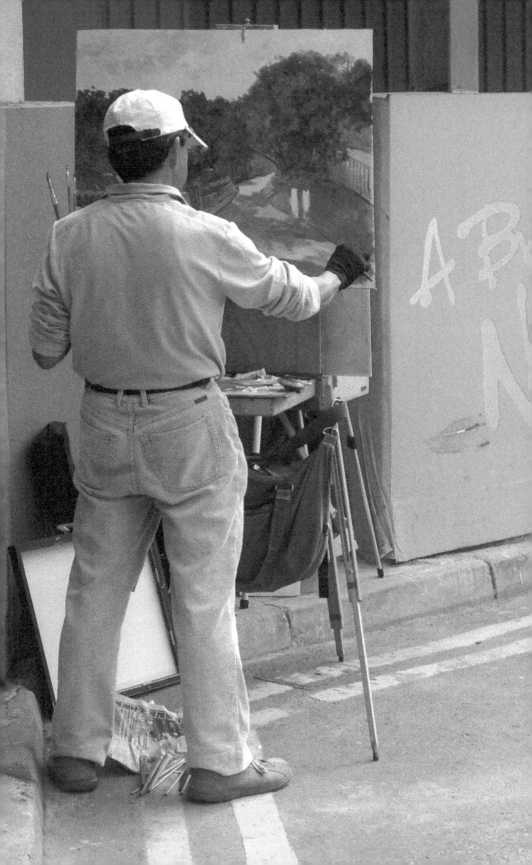

The Successful Fieldwork Experience

You can think of an interview as an orchestrated experience between three parties: researcher(s), teammate(s), and participant(s). You want to understand how that experience unfolds for each and consider what actions to take in order to have the best possible outcomes for each. And while that's implicit throughout this entire book, in this chapter you'll learn about some specific aspects that you need to understand and plan for.

Effective Team Participation

You're familiar with the rookie trope from television and movies: they enter the team clubhouse, the hospital, the law office, the military base either bewildered and sweaty, or overconfident and arrogant. Either way, you know they are going to screw things up for everyone else, and after making a big mess will hopefully learn something of a lesson. For researchers, it's a rite of passage to have the rookie ride along with you and screw things up. Unlike TV, though, sometimes the rookie outranks you. But, also unlike TV, you have compassion, and you have the tools to help the rookie be successful. Here you'll take a proactive approach in creating a positive and effective experience where—regardless of experience level—everyone on the team contributes and everyone on the team learns.

Preparing Your Colleagues for Fieldwork

It's crucial that everyone going into the field understands their roles and that the two or three people who are meeting participants will act in concert, performing like a team. Typically, I convene a brief in-person or telephone meeting where all the potential fieldwork attendees come together to review some basic rules. I'm not trying to make instant expert interviewers out of these folks; rather, I'm looking to pass along the minimum amount of information to ensure that these interviews are successful. By handing out the following guide[1] and talking through it, I am starting a conversation about expectations and roles.

---

1   Also available as a PDF at https://portigal.com/participating

A Guide to Participating in Fieldwork

Thanks for joining our research team in the field. Your participation in this part of the process will benefit the overall results of our collaboration.

Planning for the Interview

- [Information about how to sign up for the interviews.]
- Make note of the details (interview location, parking suggestion, pre-meeting time and location, participant details, etc.). If something changes with the participant's availability, we will let you know.
- Share your mobile phone info [*in the sign-up form*]; this is essential if someone is late, lost, or some other last-minute issue arises.
- Bring a digital camera or a nondigital way to take notes (no laptops or phones, please).
- Use the pre-meeting location as a last-minute chance to eat/drink/ bathroom.
- Casual dress; no logos that suggest an employer.
- No phone calls, texting, etc. during interview. Step outside if you have an emergency!

The Interview Itself

While fieldwork may appear on the surface to be a straightforward conversation, you will soon see that a lot more is going on. We don't expect you to be an expert interviewer, although you'll find that you get better with practice. Here are a few tips to help you get the most out of your experience and help us work together better:

- We'll introduce ourselves as the research team. One of us will be the **lead interviewer**. You will be the **second interviewer**. The lead interviewer runs the interview. They also coordinate the participation of the second interviewer.
- **Stay engaged!** Even if you are not asking questions, listen actively. That means thinking about what you are hearing, making eye contact, nodding affirmatively, and taking notes. You aren't just a "fly on the wall"—you are participating.
- Interviews are different from conversation. We'll use a relaxed tone, but we are purposefully guiding the interaction, often thinking several questions ahead. Although you may not see the path the lead interviewer is on, as the second interviewer, **it's important not to interject** in a way that can interrupt the flow.

continues

A Guide to Participating in Fieldwork
(continued)

- Write down and hold your questions for the appropriate time. **Interviews unfold like the chapters of a book.** Your questions need to stay within those chapters. It's the job of the lead interviewer to move the interview from one chapter to the next. The lead interviewer will make opportunities—usually at the ends of these chapters—for you to ask questions.

- **We aren't the experts.** The people we are interviewing are the experts. We want to gather their stories and opinions, and to hear what they have to say without influencing them. Use their language and terminology. If they refer to a product, brand, or feature inaccurately, don't correct them explicitly or implicitly.

- **Use open-ended questions.** Don't presume what you think the answer should be.

  Less Good: "What are three things you liked about using the bus?"

  Good: "Can you tell me about your experience using the bus?"

  Better: "Do you use public transportation?"

After the Interview

Leave some time afterward to debrief, probably around food nearby. We'll talk about our thoughts, what surprised us, and other observations. While one interview doesn't reveal a theme or a pattern, as the study proceeds, we may start to discuss what is coming up.

We can get any images or other files from you during this debrief as well.

At the end of each day or thereabouts, we'll send out highlights for each of the interviews so everyone can hear a little bit about what's been happening. If you want to add your own thoughts to the thread, we'd love that!

Keep the Field Team Lean

Generally speaking, I find the ideal size for the field team to be two people: one to lead the interview and one to back up the other person. However, it's frequently important to expose as many people as possible directly to users, so you might ask more people to join the sessions. From a social psychology perspective, we know that even the presence of others will influence behavior, so be cautious. Even three interviewers will shift the power dynamic and make some participants feel awkward and less open. This is especially true in a home environment and can be exacerbated, depending on the age and gender of the people involved. If I'm asked to field a team of three, I make sure that everyone is aware of the trade-off we're making between more team exposure and less open interviews. I'm extremely resistant to anything larger.

Everyone Stays Engaged

Another approach I've seen is to assign explicit roles (such as notetaker, photographer, videographer, and so on). I am suspicious that this is partly busywork, akin to giving a toddler a complex toy to play with so they don't get distracted during a long car ride. It is efficient to distribute key tasks, but it's also easier for someone to be successful at more well-defined roles like *photographer* versus *second interviewer*. When we meet before the interview (say, 30 minutes before, at a nearby café), I will explore that person's comfort and interest with any of the various roles.

When you are with a less experienced interviewer, you need to maintain control over the flow of the interview, while facilitating this attendee to have a successful experience. By setting expectations, they'll ideally contribute questions you wouldn't think to ask and learn more by being more actively involved.

One executive asked me hesitantly about joining in the fieldwork, promising that he'd just be there to observe and wouldn't be involved. But this isn't surgery; it's an engagement with another (conscious) person. I told him that his participation was at least welcome, and at best necessary, but his role would be an active one, even if it was mostly active listening.

There are a number of techniques for managing the second interviewer and their understandably naïve impulse to ask whatever question they think of at the moment they think of it. You can provide them with sticky notes to write their questions on as they think of them (so even if the asking is deferred, at least capturing the question provides some—albeit muted—immediate gratification). You can set aside a period of time at the end of the entire interview for their questions (although this may be asking them to "hold it" for a long period of time, and you may observe some squirming; further, the questions are perhaps decreasingly relevant as the interview proceeds). You can set aside a time for them to ask questions within each topic area before you move along, asking them "Is there anything that we've talked about so far that you'd like to know more about?" I tell my fieldwork attendees that we can have a brief conversation in front of the participant about any questions they have; they may want to suggest a topic to me rather than constructing the question directly themselves, which enables me to pick that question up or defer it as I choose. (For example, "Steve, I'd love to learn about how Jacob sends the documents to accounting.")

If you are out in the field with a peer, and you've had a fair amount of experience, not only individually but also as a team, you will find a lovely fluidity between the two of you. Your brain will tell you, based on body language and breath, when your colleague wants to ask a question. If you are chasing down a bit of information, don't turn it over immediately; just make eye contact to acknowledge that you know your partner has a question, but you're not ready for it yet. Finish the thread you are exploring, and then give them the "nod" to step in. This can be a wonderful moment, where instead of feeling like you are managing precocious toddlers, you are instead gigging with a very tight jam band. With a peer, your goal is to harness their keen brain and make the interview better. Talk to your peer before the interview and explore tactically how flexible you both want to be.

Manage Bias

Researchers—especially those new to the practice—often express concerns about bias. The fact the word connotes racism and discrimination no doubt adds to their anxiety. Certainly, there are opportunities to do better with inclusion[2] and equity[3] in research, but here the context for considering bias is usually *cognitive biases*, the ways in which our brains unconsciously drive us to think, decide, and even act irrationally.

There are hundreds of cognitive biases,[4] such as confirmation bias (where you pay more attention to information that confirms a previous belief than one that challenges) and hindsight bias (where you more confidently identify the causes of an event after it's occurred).

---

2   For example, Megan Campos, "What Did I Miss? The Hidden Costs of Deprioritizing Diversity in User Research," May 7, 2021, www.youtube.com/watch?v=E41q8Nx67Do

3   Like this interview with Sarah Fathallah in Tony Ho Tran, "Every Space Is Political," *People Nerds*, https://dscout.com/people-nerds/sarah-fathallah

4   Buster Benson organized them into key categories at https://betterhumans.pub/cognitive-bias-cheat-sheet-55a472476b18; also see the popular visualization by John Manoogian III at the same link.

One analysis[5] boils these down to a few key beliefs that unconsciously drive all of us:

- My experience is a reasonable reference.
- I make correct assessments of the world.
- I am good.
- My group is a reasonable reference.
- My group members are good.
- People's characteristics shape outcomes.

These beliefs are not always true—that's where they become biases, a flawed way of assessing the available information. Some of these biases affect how you engage with new information and how you judge other people. In user research, both the interviewer and the participant are humans who are susceptible to these biases.

Much of the guidance for individuals to overcome their own biases emphasizes mindset. Ultimately, this is hard-wired stuff, but you have agency here. Being aware that biases even exist and cultivating your own humility, curiosity, and reflectiveness are good (if vague) areas to focus on.

In research, one thing that counteracts bias is the very positive feeling—almost joyous—in realizing that you're wrong, that you had an assumption coming into the interview, one that you didn't even know you had. But after an interaction or looking at some evidence, you feel those assumptions drifting away, and you feel lighter and freer. You're realizing you have a bias, but the act of realizing that bias is also the act of letting it go. In some ways, that's what research is—the shedding of biases. You can only be so much of a hollow vessel and just exist in a state of not knowing things. You'll always have assumptions about how a task is being performed, or what a value proposition is, or how a word is being used to describe a set of experiences. Uncovering those biases and letting them go can be joyous and lead to the "aha!" moments we're looking for in this work.[6]

---

5   A. Oeberst and R. Imhoff, "Toward Parsimony in Bias Research: A Proposed Common Framework of Belief-Consistent Information Processing for a Set of Biases," *Perspectives on Psychological Science*, (March 2023).

6   Adapted from a wide-ranging conversation about bias and other aspects of user research, Carrie Neill, "Finding the 'Aha!' Moment," *People Nerds*, https://dscout.com/people-nerds/steve-portigal-bias-in-research

David Dylan Thomas[7] advises that in user research interviews, people can't properly remember their rationale for past decisions, and thus asking about hypotheticals (e.g., "Although you did take Action A, did you consider doing Action B?") is a way to surface more accurate motivations.

He also explains how people are bad at accurately predicting their future behavior (say, their use of a product that doesn't yet exist that is being proposed in a research session), partly because any question about the future will be answered based on the participant's feelings about the present. The present is the dominant context that you must factor in when interpreting any answer about the future.

In her talk about cognitive biases and user research,[8] Zsuzsa Kovács suggests that researchers should work in pairs and give each other feedback so that each researcher might serve as a counterpoint to the other's individual cognitive biases. She also points out that open-ended conversation, like in an interview, can be less biased than a survey, where the questions are decided ahead of time, and that questions about specifics will produce more accurate responses. As well, conducting research in someone's environment (versus your own office or a facility) can anchor participants more effectively in their past actions and help deliver more accurate responses.

> **NOTE** NEVER SAY NEVER AGAIN
>
> Too often, guidance for interviewing users advises people to "never" do something: Never ask about the future, never ask how much someone would pay, never ask hypothetical questions, never ask why, and so on. While those remonstrations are punchy, they are missing some words, like "...if you expect the response to be reliable on its face."
>
> You should ask someone how much they would pay, not so you can get a read on the price-point the product should sell at, but rather to reveal more about their underlying mental models for price and value. You should ask someone how they think their children will experience something differently than they are, not for an accurate prediction for the next generation, but as a

---

7   David Dylan Thomas, *Design for Cognitive Bias* (New York: A Book Apart, 2020).

8   Zsuzsa Kovács, "The Problems in Your Head—How Cognitive Biases Affect Your Research," WebExpo, June 10, 2022.

different way of exploring your participant's mental model for today. Your goal is to facilitate meaningful reflection and consideration that you will analyze and synthesize (see Chapter 9, "Making Sense of Your Data"); it isn't to extract a litany of facts and truths. Ask all sorts of questions but be aware of how you should understand the responses.

Planning for Remote Research

We've been conducting user research remotely for a long time. (Nate Bolt and Tony Tulathimutte wrote a book about remote research[9] in 2010!) But when COVID-19 locked down much of the world, remote became the only way to safely do user research. It became apparent that using an online platform like Zoom or Google Meet or Microsoft Teams for research offers additional opportunities to engage coworkers in participation, but not without some challenges. The risk, as Research Operations manager Neil Santiago explained, is that "It's tempting to just run your sessions like your typical online meetings, but including all your potential observers on the call can be counterproductive. When the session experience feels more like being on stage than a typical conversation, you can expect some participants to get more guarded about sharing criticism, expressing unpolished ideas, and admitting confusion."

One solution, the specifics depending on your platform and plan, is to set up a live stream, view-only version of the call. While the researchers and participant are having the interview in one "room," other people can watch the session while it's happening. These folks don't show up as participants in the actual interview session, and they aren't able to speak or chat in the interview itself (see Figure 4.1). In this "back room," observers can come and go at any time.

---

9 "Nate Bolt and Tony Tulathimutte, *Remote Research: Real Users, Real Time, Real Research* (New York: Rosenfeld Media, 2010). https://rosenfeldmedia.com/books/remote-research/

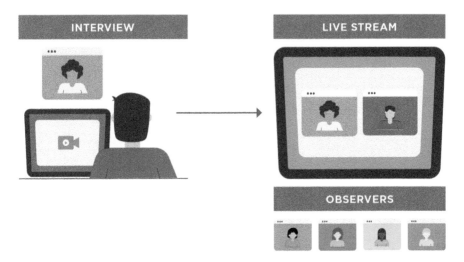

FIGURE 4.1

Configure remote live streaming so that researchers, participants, and observers each have the relevant view of the session.

Setting up these platforms and technologies so that things run smoothly for all of the different parties takes a bit of operations work to configure, but it's worth the effort. As Neil advised, "If your calendar invites to session observers are filled with warnings like 'Be sure to mute both audio and video! Don't use the chat!' or you've had to interrupt sessions to give these instructions, know that you're just discouraging attendance. Pointing observers to a live stream lets them engage stress-free and acknowledges that they may miss instructions, be late, leave early, or get distracted during the sessions for totally valid reasons."

You want a good experience for your colleagues and your participant, as well as making it easier for you to focus. With a "back-room" approach, you should tell your participant that other people are listening in, just like you're going to reconfirm that you are recording the interview, and so on.

Ideally, with a virtual "back room," one of the interviewers will be on-screen, in the session with the participant, but also monitoring the comments and questions from observers. Sometimes teams will designate a separate place to chat (such as a Slack thread) rather than doing this in the video program itself, so that the conversation persists after the session ends.

The researcher leading the interview should not be expected to troubleshoot technical issues that colleagues in the back room are experiencing. The researcher shouldn't be expected to monitor the back-room chat either; the chat will be a conversation, not just requests to ask specific questions (which, anyway, sometimes need clarification).

Some researchers are more comfortable with multitasking, but your primary focus should be on the conversation with your participant. Switching focus between windows (say, looking from Zoom to Slack) will be visible to your participant and will suggest that you aren't paying full attention. If you are reading through a thread in that window to find requests or questions, your focus on your subject will be compromised.

Another aspect to consider is how you use your calendar program to manage and communicate the details of the interview (see Figure 4.2). A calendar event will typically contain the link to the meeting, as well as a list of participants, their email addresses, and the name of the meeting. In some cases, you don't want other people in the organization to know the names of your participants or their contact information. If your colleagues have access to the link for the interview *and* the link for the back room, there's always a risk they'll join the wrong session.

FIGURE 4.2

This calendar invite—for the live stream room and not the interview itself—is for the internal team, not the participant.

As well, your calendar invite will have a title. If you are sending this invite to your participant, it should not only make sense to them but also reinforce their importance. If your team at MangoTech is interviewing chemical engineers, "Interview with MangoTech" is better for them. "Interview with ChemEng 1" may be better for you and your colleagues but is confusing if not disrespectful to your interviewee. Maybe "Interview: MangoTech & Totally Chemical." In addition, take the time to create an event description that makes sense for everyone's calendar.

Another bit of operations magic is to create a separate calendar where your colleagues can see what interviews (and associated debriefs) are taking place and how and when to join. However, just as the video call itself is a replica of the original interview, the calendar event is separate and will exclude information sent to the participant and include information relevant to them but that shouldn't be shared with the participant.

Anticipating the Key Stages of the Interview

Most people are at least conversationally familiar with the Kübler-Ross model of the five stages of grief: denial, anger, bargain, depression, and acceptance. This model describes a consistent set of elements in a very human experience. At the same time, Kübler-Ross pointed out that people don't necessarily experience *all* those stages or experience them in that particular order.

A contrasting model is the *beat sheet* (see Figure 4.3)—a tool for screenwriters that lays out the necessary sections of a typical three-act screenplay, a ubiquitous structure for Hollywood films. There are even beat-sheet calculators that will take the number of pages of a screenplay as input and identify on what specific pages the different story elements should appear. While Kübler-Ross is descriptive, beat sheets are predictive. While being predictive might seem a limitation when making movies, this consistent structure and the reliance on other tropes is part of what makes movies work: viewers are being taught the code with every experience.

I've identified the stages that most interviews go through, and my model is somewhere between descriptive and predictive. You may notice some or all of these stages in your interviews, but you can't anticipate, for example, that one will (or should!) happen precisely at the 40-minute mark. But each stage requires specific tactical preparation or responses from you, the interviewer. Get familiar with the details of the stages, and if you don't recognize them while reading, you probably will the next time you are out in the field. As you gain experience, moving through these stages will become second nature.

THE BLAKE SNYDER BEAT SHEET

PROJECT TITLE:
GENRE:
DATE:

1. Opening Image (1):

2. Theme Stated (5):

3. Set-Up (1-10):

4. Catalyst (12):

5. Debate (12-25):

6. Break into Two (25)

7. B Story (30):

8. Fun and Games (30-55):

9. Midpoint (55):

10. Bad Guys Close In (55-75):

11. All Is Lost (75):

12. Dark Night of the Soul (75-85):

13. Break into Three (85):

14. Finale (85-110):

15. Final Image (110):

FIGURE 4.3
The beat sheet outlines a standardized structure for storytelling via a screenplay.

Once you get on-site, you'll find these different stages:

- Crossing the threshold
- Restating objectives
- Kick-off question
- Accept the awkwardness
- The tipping point
- Reflection and projection
- The soft close

In Chapter 2, "Research Logistics," I described the general flow of most interview guides. The flow of the guide corresponds roughly to the stages of the interview.

Crossing the Threshold

The very first few moments of an on-site interview are often characterized by mild confusion, especially if you are going to someone's home, and less so if you are arriving at a professional office with a reception area. In general, your participants aren't 100 percent clear on what's expected of them. They may not have been told, or remember, your name or the organization you represent, and only know the details of who recruited them to participate. Before you arrive, figure out what you are going to say. It may be as simple as "Hi, I'm Steve. I'm here for the interview." Or "Hi, I'm Steve from _____. I'm here for the interview." (These work especially well if your name happens to be Steve.)

Think carefully about what organization name you use. They may know the recruiting firm's name (or even the name of the individual recruiter), but not the name of your company. They may be more familiar with your product's name (such as YouTube) than your organization's name (such as Alphabet). Identify yourself in a way that they'll recognize. Of course, if you've personally reached out to the participants by email or telephone before the interview, this is much simpler.

Whether you are in a home, a workplace, or any other environment, once you are "in," social graces matter. Introduce the rest of your fieldwork team and offer to take off your shoes if you are in someone's home (but be sure you don't have holes in your socks!). As you come in, figure out where you want to start the session. In an office, it may be a conference room. In a home, it may be the living room or dining table. Even if the bulk of the interview is going to take place at a specific location (say, at a computer or in the mail room), you may want to start off in a more open and front-stage part of the environment. Your participant won't know what you need, so be prepared to ask them.

Arrange seating so that you and your fellow interviewer (or interviewers) are near each other. In order to maximize the engagement among all parties, you want the fieldwork team to be able to maintain eye contact with the participant, and you want the participant to be able to respond to questions from either of you without having to turn their head too far (see Figure 4.4). If need be, ask the participant to sit in a particular spot. The participant doesn't know what's supposed to happen, so by gently taking charge, you can reassure them and set the tone for the whole interview.

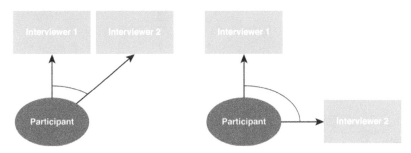

FIGURE 4.4
Ensure that all interviewers can maintain eye contact with the participant (L), rather than forcing them to swivel their head to keep you both in view (R).

If you're shooting video, make sure that the lighting is appropriate. If your participant is sitting in front of a bright light (such as a window), then ask them to move or close a blind. If the room is too dark, ask about opening window coverings or turning on lights. If there's a radio or television on, ask them to turn it off (as sometimes those can appear more prominently on audio recordings than you would expect). This isn't a social visit (as a guest, you probably wouldn't ask your friend to move to a different seat), but rather it's a purposeful, arranged session. If you are offered a drink, feel free to accept it, as this is the participant's way of anchoring the session to a familiar scenario. The participant isn't trained as a professional interviewee so they will, of course, rely on familiar styles of social interactions. Although it's fine for you to accept their social gestures (in some cases, it can be essential, because a failure to do so can be read as rude, so err on the side of taking the offered glass of water), as the interviewer, you will offer fewer of those gestures yourself.

As you are settling into place and getting your gear unpacked and set up, ask the participant to sign any nondisclosure and consent agreements. I'll often bring it up as quickly as possible and tell the participant "Before we get started, we've just got some paperwork for you." The key words here are "Before we get started." Specifics will vary depending on the study, but in general, ethically and legally, the interview shouldn't start until your participant has signed whatever forms you've planned for. I prefer to hand over a pen and the forms and then sit quietly (or prepare my surroundings) while they read it over. Defensive nattering ("Ha, ha, this won't end up on YouTube") undercuts the document's clarity and raises concerns that the participant might not even have. Start setting up the video camera or getting your field materials ready rather than watching the participant.

> **NOTE** INFORMED CONSENT
>
> The well-established ethical standards for *informed consent* emphasize the difference between obtaining a signature on a form (essentially meeting a legal requirement) versus taking responsibility for the person signing the form clearly agreeing to the specifics about their participation. This means going over the document with the participant to ensure that they understand the goals of the study, what is expected of them, and any possible risks or benefits they might face by participating. It could also include reminding them of their right to decline to participate at the outset or at any point, and information about what data will be stored, how, and for how long.
>
> A team from Sesame Workshop created a set of videos to help better facilitate informed consent.[10] IDEO describes how they adapted their consent process for Chinese cultures,[11] where people may find signing a document to be intimidating, especially before they've established rapport. They take time at the beginning to explain the specifics but defer asking for a signature until the conclusion of the interview.

Sometimes the people who join me in the field will try to fill these initial moments (especially if they see me busy with the equipment) with small talk that can inadvertently transition into some of the interview content itself. The participant—without a clear sense of the process (remember the "before we get started")—may start offering up opinions and details. Agree ahead of time with your colleagues

---

10 The Muppet videos are at www.youtube.com/watch?v=hYNbCIRb2uI&list=PLETVq3OFVKVsFwRd0MVtrHGYh6-DFhSXx and were built on other work using video to support consent in low-literacy contexts. Kim Foulds, Joyce Rafla, and Tareq Sharawi, "Using Muppets to Demystify Informed Consent," Sesame Workshop Cooney Center, June 6, 2022, https://joanganzcooneycenter.org/wp-content/uploads/2022/06/jgcc_muppets_informed_consent.pdf

11 IDEO, *The Little Book of Design Research Ethics*, 2015, https://page.ideo.com/lbodre

not to let the small talk turn into questioning before you have the signed consent, and before you have your video camera (or other recording media) turned on. Otherwise, you're going to have to ask those questions again. Small talk is a lovely lubricant but keep it to small talk—discuss the weather, or how your day is going, but don't start asking questions about artifacts in the environment or how long they have been doing their job.

Restating Objectives

This is the point at which the interview itself really begins. Thank the participant for taking the time to speak with you, and at a high level, tell them what this is about. This is an early and important chance for you to speak using their terminology, not yours. Depending on how their participation was secured, someone may have told them something about why you are doing this research and what is being asked of them. If that someone wasn't you, you don't really know what was said. Even if it was you who spoke with the participant, you don't really know what they took away from the conversation.

It's okay to describe your work as "market research" if that's the most understandable way for the participant to know what you are doing. The differences between user research and design research and market research do not matter to them! I refer to our process and objectives at a high level: "We're working for a technology company, and we're out talking to a bunch of different people about how they are using their laptops." Generally, you should avoid describing yourself as a "user experience researcher" or describing your interview as a "research session" that you are "moderating" or tell them that you're "speaking to different personas." While you may be seeking to establish credibility with professional-sounding language, this unfamiliar jargon can feel alienating.

Provide context for the interview but keep it very short. You're trying to get the interview going by setting it up with just enough context and then getting out of the way. You shouldn't be holding the floor by talking about yourself, your organization, and your project. This type of information doesn't add relevant context for the person you're speaking with.

If you reveal either your business objective or research questions in this part of the interview, your participant may assume that's your invitation to begin answering *those* questions specifically, versus your carefully plotted-out interview guide. Sometimes you can roll with that and redirect them, but there's the risk that your redirection embarrasses them for jumping into what they presumed you wanted to know.

For example, contrast

> Thanks for speaking with us today, I'm Steve, and I'm a Senior User Researcher with the MangoTech UX department, and I'll be moderating this session. As you may know, for this project we're researching with a range of personas in the industry to learn about their tactics and needs and behaviors and best practices for doing their jobs as we plan our integration rollout and top-down segmentation for Q4.

versus

> Thanks for speaking with us today, I'm Steve from MangoTech, and we're just talking with different people about how they use their laptops.

I sometimes acknowledge the recruiting process explicitly. Depending on the topic, it may have been very clear to the participant by the end of the screening interview what it was we are interested in, saying, "You probably know from the questions that we were asking when you talked with ... that we're interested in ... " or "I don't know how much you know about what we're doing. I know you answered a lot of questions about ... "

Let the participant know what to expect by giving a thumbnail outline of the process: "We'll take about 90 minutes with you. We've got a bunch of questions to ask to start off, and then later it'd be great if you can show us the warehouse," or "Let's start here with some discussion, and then we've got something we'd like to show you and get your feedback." If they have any concerns ("I have to stop at 2:15 to go pick up my daughter"; "Ummm.... I didn't know you were going to look in our kitchen, it's kind of messy"), then these should come up right away, and you can adjust your process, timing, or clarify your expectations. This has the additional benefit of reminding your client (who maybe isn't as prepared as you'd like) what is going to happen.

Engage your participant: "Do you have any questions for us before we begin?" If they don't have questions, keep moving, because even though you've told them that you have specific questions for them, a participant may feel that it's up to them to somehow start telling what they think might address your objectives. You may even want to shut down too many detailed questions ("How many people are you meeting?" "What company do you work for?") by deferring those until the end of the interview. In a gentle way, you can use this to further set the tone for you as the leader of the interview.

NOTE TRUE TO YOUR WORD

> Some researchers feel it's important to tell their participant at the outset that "there are no wrong answers" or "we just want your honest feedback." What's much more important is how you follow through on that promise. The way you act throughout the interview (including listening and establishing rapport) is how you create a safe space. You want the participant to share information without risk of judgment, but simply uttering this disclaimer at the beginning is entirely ineffective. You must actually model the promise through your own behavior. In Chapter 5, "Best Practices for Interviewing," I'll go into detail about listening to participants and building rapport.

FROM MY PERSPECTIVE

POWER-SHARING AGREEMENT

Once, in interviews with some high-powered, fast-talking finance professionals, I found myself getting through about half of these first few sentences before they verbally brushed past me and launched into their complaints about our client's product (something we were all well aware of and not at all focused on for these interviews). Because of the difficulty of access to these customers (who were basically doing the interview as a favor), they didn't seem to have well-managed expectations about our goals. Eventually, I just turned this part of the interview over to them, kicking off by asking, "Well, before we start, why do *you* think we're here?" Inevitably, they politely raged about their current frustrations until I could interrupt with "Actually, we know that's important, but that's not what we're hoping to talk about today."

Since that experience, I often begin interviews with some variation of this approach "Thanks for agreeing to speak with me. What are your expectations for this conversation?" Now the participant is answering questions right at the very beginning, and they have a stake in the session itself. I don't usually need to radically reframe the interview objectives; often, I respond with a "yes, and..."[12] clarification—"Yes, that's right, and we'll probably focus mostly today on your actual setup that you've already built." ▄

---

12 A principle from improv that can be applied in many interpersonal contexts. Rather than disagreeing with someone's idea and sharing yours instead ("No, but..."), you accept their suggestion and build on it. It reframes a potential disagreement into a collaboration.

Kick-Off Question

This is another transitional moment as you move into the body of the interview and begin to actively inhabit the role of the question-asker. Your intro words—"So, to start"—help move things forward, past small talk and logistics. The first question is usually a simple broad one to set some context.

"Maybe introduce yourself and tell us about what your job is here?" It doesn't matter too much what the question is because you are going to follow it up with many more specific questions. The key here is not to start too specifically ("Ahem. Question 1. What are the top features you desire in your mobile device?"), but to be mindful of shifting into the mode of asking questions.

Accept the Awkwardness

As you proceed through your questions, you may encounter some resistance. Although many people (especially those likely to agree to participate) will be extroverted and comfortable, some people will be uncomfortable. There's no formula for how long it takes people to get past discomfort. Some people will get there with you in a few minutes, whereas others may take an hour. Sometimes (rarely, in my experience), they'll never reach that point. This discomfort presents itself in subtle ways; rather than frowns and squirming, you may observe stiff posture and clipped deliberate responses. They may fend off your questions (while seemingly answering them) by implying that those are not normal things to be asking about, or providing little or no detail about themselves, describing their behavior as "you know, just regular."

You may have to identify your own feelings of discomfort to know when you're in this stage. If you feel like you don't have permission to keep going, or that this person doesn't really want you there, you are in this stage. First, you have to accept this as awkward. It's not the worst thing in the world to be conversing with someone and feeling ill at ease. You aren't in physical peril; it's just an inner feeling. Let it happen, but don't let it define you. Listen to the feeling and set it aside.

Now give your participant plenty of ways to succeed. Ask them short and easy questions, keeping the inquiry factual, straightforward, and simple. This isn't the time to ask challenging questions or to bring out props or stimuli. Be patient and keep asking questions and keep accepting, acknowledging, and appreciating their responses. Your own comfort (or discomfort) will come through and contribute to the tone. If you're following your interview guide linearly, you may get a good portion of the way through in a short time and begin to feel some panic about the number of questions you've come with. Just stick with it; the remaining questions will take longer to get through (and will generate more follow-up questions, too).

> **NOTE** HOLD ON TO YOUR LOOSE-LEAF
>
> When you're interviewing in-person, your interview guide should be printed on paper. Don't try to lead an interview using a document on your phone! Keep your printout in a portfolio, a folder, a sheaf of papers, a notebook, or something else. You'll be better off if the guide appears to be put away when you aren't using it. Early in my career, I did an interview with the guide held out in front of me as my only bit of "business." At one point, my participant snatched it from my hands and said, "Okay, what else do you wanna know?" Although this is unlikely to happen often, it served as a good lesson for me to tote my paraphernalia in a more professional (and protected) manner.

The Tipping Point

Although you can't predict when it will happen, there's often a visceral point in the interview when the participant shifts from giving short answers to telling stories (see Figure 4.5). Whether or not it's an actual moment where the answers get longer, there is a point where you realize that you've arrived at a high level of rapport and the tenor of the exchange is different. In all likelihood, by the time you have that realization, you've probably been crossing back and forth between short answers and stories.

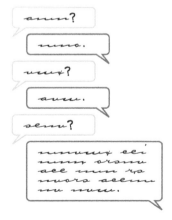

FIGURE 4.5
You can see where this hypothetical interview tips from questions and answers into stories.

Even if you do encounter more short answers, you are on your way, so just stick with what you've been doing. Stories are where the richest insights lie, and your objective is to get to this point in every interview. The thing about this tipping point is that you don't know when it's coming. You have to be patient in the question-and-answer part of the interview because you don't always feel that what you're doing to build rapport is actually getting anywhere. You have to trust in the process, which becomes easier with experience.

Reflection and Projection

The deepest rapport comes when the participant has spent enough time immersed in the topic in a supportive and exploratory fashion. By this time, you've presumably captured many of the details around process, behaviors, usage, and so on, and are ready to move into the higher-level part of the inquiry. Now your participant is thinking about the big picture. Their responses drift into sweeping statements about themselves, their goals, their dreams, their past, the future, our society, and so on. This can be the most fun part of the interview— it's certainly the most inspiring. You are now fully drawn into their world, and they are painting a detailed picture of what lies beneath or what lies beyond.

Just because people are speaking about a future (say, how self-driving cars will change how they go on vacation) doesn't mean it's an accurate prediction. That's not the point of the question; it's what these predictions and reflections reveal. These parts of the interview often produce phrases or ideas that the field team will continue to repeat and go back to, as they distill complex issues into visionary notions.

The Soft Close

Assuming that your participant isn't running off to another appointment, the winding down of the interview can be a soft process. In Chapter 2, I recommended asking participants if there was anything that they think we should know. This question doesn't automatically reveal some previously hidden gem, but your participant, without specifically being prompted, might summarize or reflect back on the key points they want you to take away. You can also ask it directly if you think it might be helpful.

This question begins to shift the dynamic into "wrapping up." Even after that, the more explicit cues (thanking them, handing them the incentive, packing up your stuff, standing up) may not mean they are going to stop talking. Physicians and therapists are familiar with the "doorknob phenomenon," where crucial information is revealed just as the patient is about to depart. So, consider keeping your recording device on. Even as you are heading to the door, the interview may resume, at the participant's initiative. Or you may see something in the environment to ask about. Keep your eyes and brain in interview mode until you are fully departed. Even if you are tired and ready to leave, stifle the inner "Oh, there's nothing here" voice that wants you to pull the plug. Stick with it a couple of minutes more. Those may be the bits of recorded data that pull the whole project together for you in the analysis phase. You don't know at this point!

The Last Word

Although interviews are all wonderfully unique, they tend to follow a consistent pattern. Each stage requires specific tactical preparation or responses from you, the interviewer. With experience, moving through the different stages will become second nature.

- If you are joined by colleagues who aren't skilled at interviewing, give them tasks (for example, photographing the interview) or brief them on when to ask questions and what kind of questions they should ask.

- When you first come in, set up your seating so that the participant can easily maintain eye contact with *all* interviewers. Use just enough small talk but don't get bogged down in chat. If you are offered a drink, feel free to accept it.

- Start with a general, easy question (such as asking the participant to introduce themself). Ideally, the rest of the interview just flows from there as follow-up questions.

- If your participant exhibits discomfort, you can choose whether or not you feel discomfort yourself in response. If you feel uncomfortable, you should find a way to accept that feeling as just a feeling and move forward.

- People will respond with short answers at first and will eventually reach a point where they are telling stories. You can't predict how long it will take to reach that point, but that *is* the goal.

- Remember the "doorknob phenomenon," where people suddenly open up as the session ends. Try to keep recording until you're out the door.

CHAPTER 5

Best Practices
for Interviewing

W hen Wayne Gretzky apocryphally[1] explained his hockey success as "I don't skate to where the puck is, I skate to where the puck is going to be," he identified a key characteristic of many experts: the underlying *framework* that drives everything. This platonically idealized Gretzky could have revealed any number of tactics, such as his grip or the way he shifts his weight when he skates. On another note, Keith Richards explains his guitar sound, which involves removing the 6th string, tuning to open G, and using a particular fretting pattern, as "five strings, three notes, two fingers, and one asshole." Even though Keith is explaining the tactics, he's also revealing something ineffable about where he's coming from. The higher-level operating principles that drive these experts are compelling and illustrative.

Expert researchers also have their own operating principles. In this chapter, I'll outline four fundamentals: checking your worldview at the door, embracing other people's vision, building rapport, and listening. As you develop, the process evolves from *a toolkit for asking questions* into *a way of being*, and you'll find that many of the tactical problems to solve in interviewing are simply no-brainers.

Check Your Worldview at the Door

I've been asked, "What was the most surprising thing you ever learned while doing fieldwork?" I scratch my head over that one because I don't go out into the field with a very strong point of view. Of course, I'm informed by my own experiences, my suspicions, and what the project stakeholders have told me, but I approach the interviews with a sense of what I can only call a *bland curiosity*.

As the researcher, it's my responsibility to find out what's going on. I'm not invested in a particular outcome. Even more (and this is where the blandness comes from), I'm not fully invested in a specific set of answers. Sure, we've got specific things we want to learn—questions we *have* to answer in order to fulfill our brief. But my hunger to learn from my participant is broad, not specific. I'm curious, but I don't know yet what I'm curious about. My own expectations are muted, blunted, and distributed. Although I will

---

1   In fact, it was Walter Gretzky, Wayne's dad, who said it, as "Go to where the puck is going, not where it has been." Jill Rosenfeld, "CDU to Gretzky: The Puck Stops Here!" Fast Company, Consultant Debunking Unit, July 2000, www.fastcompany.com/40565/cdu-gretzky-puck-stops-here

absolutely find the information I'm tasked with uncovering, I also bring a general curiosity. Now, the people I work with don't have the luxury of bland curiosity. Whether they are marketers, product managers, engineers, or designers (or even other researchers), they often have their own beliefs about what is going on with people. This makes sense: If there's enough organizational momentum to convene a research project, someone has been thinking hard about the issues and the opportunities, and has come to a point of view.

The Brain Dump

At the beginning of the project, you should convene a brain dump with your team. Ask yourselves: "What do you expect to hear in the interviews?" "What do you hope to hear in the interviews?" Take what's in everyone's heads and make it explicit (see Figure 5.1). Whether it's face-to-face, in front of a whiteboard, or remotely in a shared document, talk through assumptions, expectations, closely held beliefs, perspectives, and hypotheses. Contradictions are inevitable and should even be encouraged. You shouldn't negotiate or debate between different responses—just capture it all. The point is not establishing consensus: it's to surface what's implicit. By saying it aloud and writing it down, the issues leave the group specifically and enter an external, neutral space.

FIGURE 5.1
Capture everything that everyone thinks they know so that it's not stuck in their heads.

It's also not about being right or wrong; don't attribute people's contributions (and you can even take steps to anonymize all the input) so that people feel more confident expressing themselves. You shouldn't go back and validate the brain dump against the resulting data. The objective of this activity is to shake loose what is in your mind and free you to see new things. Think about it as a transitional ritual of unburdening, like people setting down their keys, phone, purse, wallet, and other accessories as soon as they return home (Figure 5.2).

FIGURE 5.2
Transitional rituals are actions we take to remind ourselves that we are shifting from one mode of being to another.

Make the Interview About the Interview

Another transitional ritual is to make a small declaration to yourself and your fellow fieldworkers in the moments before you begin an interview. If you are outside someone's apartment or entering their workspace, turn to each other and state what you are there to accomplish. If you were the hero in an action movie, you'd probably growl purposefully "Let's do this thing." Admittedly, fieldwork is rarely that glamorous, so you might want to clarify what you mean by "this thing."

Remember, even though the interviews are part of a larger corporate initiative to (say) "identify next-gen opportunities for Q3 roadmap," that's not where you should focus as you go into the interview. Set aside the underlying goals for the duration of the session. "This thing" might instead be learning about Vera and how they use their mobile device to manage their home-based business, or the process for deploying new routers at MangoTech's new campus. It's important to take that moment for yourselves to tangibly confirm—and affirm—your immediate objective.

One of my clients would bring a meditation bell out into the field (see Figure 5.3). After parking the car in front of their research participant's home, they'd go to the trunk to get their gear, sound the bell for themselves, and then go knock on the door. They explained that this ritual was a way of reminding everyone to *stay present*.

FIGURE 5.3
Meditation bells provide a specific grounding moment that separates time into "before the interview" and "at the interview."

Embrace How Other People See the World

If you've effectively purged yourself of your own worldview, you are reborn anew, merely a hollow vessel waiting to be filled with insights. Lovely image, isn't it? It's not quite accurate. You need not only to be ready to hear your participant's take on things, but you should also be *hungry* for it. This willingness to embrace is an active, deliberate state.

Go Where the People Are

Rather than asking people to come to you to be interviewed, go where they are. In order to embrace their world, you have to be in their world. Inviting them into your realm won't cut it. (And let's face it, even if a neutral market research facility isn't technically *your* realm, that's how your participants will perceive it.) You'll benefit by interviewing them in their own environment—this is the environment you are interested in, where the artifacts and behaviors you want to learn about are rooted. By the same token, you'll also benefit from your own first-hand experience in that environment. The information you learn when going into other people's worlds is different from what you learn when bringing them into yours.

To that end, try not to bring your world into theirs. Leave the company-logo clothing (and accessories) at home. Wearing your colors is fine when you're rooting for the home team or taking your hog to Sturgis, but it has no place in the interview (see Figure 5.4).

HELLS ANGELS, A CREATIVE COMMONS ATTRIBUTION (2.0)
IMAGE FROM BRIMELOW'S FLICKR PHOTOSTREAM

FIGURE 5.4
Displaying your affiliation may be appropriate in some settings, but not typically during fieldwork.

Sometimes you can't go to where the people are, and instead are connected to your participants through technology. Consider ways to mitigate some of the effects of remote research on both researchers and participants.

During an audio-only interview (telephone, or video calling with the camera off), a lack of facial cues makes it a bit harder to adjust your pace and rhythm to the participant. Experiment with giving your participant an extra beat of silence to ensure that they feel permitted to speak and to allow them to continue to speak. If silence is making them uncomfortable (you get a, "Hello? Are you there?"), pick up the pace a bit and introduce verbal handoffs (such as, "Go ahead...please continue...").

Since you won't have as much context, look for other ways to compensate (see Figure 5.5). Ask participants beforehand to send some photos of their environment or to describe elements you won't be able to see during the call. When you are arranging the interview, establish their expected location. (For example, will they be in their car in traffic, or will they be at home caring for their children?) At the same time, confirm the length of the interview because it may overlap with other activities. At the end of the interview (or right afterward), ask for photos of specific things that the participants referred to (but didn't show) during the session.

FIGURE 5.5
When the interviewer and participant can't see each other, it's anyone's guess how their contexts differ.

If you use video-calling technologies like Zoom and FaceTime, you are introducing other complicating factors:

- Your participant might not be fully proficient at using these tools. It's not ideal to begin the interview having your participant exasperated and feeling incompetent. Even if they are familiar with the technology in general, they may find shifting from (say) Zoom (their usual platform) to WebEx (what your organization uses) to be challenging. Service designer Victor Udoewa accommodates whatever device and platform his participants prefer.

- You are subject to the variability of internet connection speeds (and software reliability) on both ends. Four minutes of reconnecting and dropping calls is not acceptable, so you might arrange for a technology test before the interview.

- Not everyone is fully literate in video conferencing. Consider your audience. You might want to warm up the interview with a discussion of the communication context: "It's unfortunate we couldn't meet with you face-to-face. Do you regularly meet with people on Zoom?"

And while you can't see the full context of your participant's environment without being there, Shannon Stoll, a user researcher, draws inferences from whatever clues she can get, like where the participant joins from, if there are other people around, and if they are on their phone or laptop. She often asks participants to share their screen; it doesn't provide more context about the *physical* environment, but it offers context for how a digital tool is used. Victor Udoewa asks participants for a guided tour of their space, arranging for the interview to be over a mobile phone instead of a harder-to-carry-around laptop.

Asking Questions When You *Think* You Know the Answer

You already know how *you* plan a balanced meal, prepare your taxes, or disable motion smoothing on your smart TV. You may have an idea about how your participant does those things (because of what you've learned about them during the screening process, or implied by something they said earlier in the interview, or assumed by what you've seen other people do in the past). However, you need to be open to asking for details anyway. I'll have more in the next chapter about asking questions, but for now keep in mind that to embrace their world you need to explore the details of their world.

Some interviewers fear that they are being false by asking a question if they think they know the answer. I've watched less-experienced researchers affect a higher-pitched tone of voice as they struggle to perform as sincerely curious. But it's easier and more effective to acknowledge that your presumptions are simply that and to allow yourself to be curious. What's more authentic than being uncertain how your participant is going to answer a particular question? Interesting tidbits can emerge when you ask these questions, as this hypothetical example suggests:

Question: When are your taxes due?

The answer (which you already know): April 15

The response you fear: Why are you asking me this stuff? Everyone knows that it's April 15. Get out of my house, jerk face!

The type of answer you are just as likely to get if you swallow your discomfort and ask the question anyway: I always complete everything by March 1. I *think* it's April 15 this year, but I never really pay attention to that.

The goal here is to make it clear to the participant (and to yourself) that they are the expert and you are the novice. This definitely pays off. When I conduct research outside of North America, people tangibly extend themselves to answer my necessarily naïve questions. Respect for their expertise coupled with your own humility serves as a powerful invitation to your interviewee.

This points to a challenge in interviewing someone you know well (say, a friend or coworker). Even if it's easier to get them to participate than a "stranger," you have a much higher level of "stuff you already actually know about them," so asking questions about those topics gets awkward. Imagine asking if they travel for work when you *just* looked after their cat for their work trip. Instead of embracing their world, you are pushed to start with what you already know (and that they know that you know, because you've shared it).

Nip Distractions in the Bud

Tactically, make sure that you are not distracted when you arrive. Take care of your food, drink, and restroom needs in advance. When I meet up with colleagues who are coming to the interview from a different location, we pick an easy location (such as a Starbucks) for a pre-interview briefing. It gives us time to shift into a calm and focused interview mindset, review the participant's profile, catch up on what's been happening in the field to date, and address our personal needs. If your brain is chattering, "Lord, am I famished! When's lunch?" you are at a disadvantage when it comes to tuning in to what's going on in the interview.

Needless to say, silence your mobile phone and don't plan on taking calls or checking messages during the interview. I say "needless," because I met a team that took a different approach. Sensitive to the commitment their internal clients were making in leaving the office for fieldwork, they allowed mobile device usage during the interview, within limits. Although they were inspired by one colleague who had the stealth check-below-the-table move down cold, most people weren't able to handle it quite so deftly. It was a good lesson to learn; they won't be allowing mobile phones in the future. Mind you, even if one were successfully stealthy, that's beside the point. Figure 5.6 is an evocative depiction of the multitasking potential of technology, but during an interview (and probably during a date), you should be fully engaged with the other person.

FIGURE 5.6
Just because you *can* multitask doesn't mean you *should*.

Build Rapport

I often leave an interview with my head slightly swimming, in a state between energized and exhausted. In addition to all the useful information that will impact the project, I've just made an intense connection with a new person. I've established a rapport with someone. That's a powerful feeling, and likely as not, my participant is feeling the same way. Our quotidian transaction to learn about breakfast making has turned into something else.

The rapport is what makes for great interviews. You won't leave every interview walking on a cloud, but getting to that state with your interviewee is something to strive for.

It's your job to develop that rapport over the course of the interview. By all means, recruit participants who are articulate, outgoing, and eager to be part of the interview, but remember that creating that connection falls to you, the interviewer.

> **NOTE** THE CHARM OFFENSIVE
>
> Some people can be effortlessly charismatic. They might be self-deprecating, sharing details about themselves. They can be funny, inducing positive emotional reactions (like smiling and laughing) in others. But when one of the interviewers has a great deal of unrestrained charm, they can draw focus and energy toward themselves. This works against what you want to accomplish in an interview. If this is one of your natural gifts, take care to leave a lot of space for your participant (and your colleagues). Or, you may find yourself interviewing alongside someone who is very effective at getting people to respond positively to them. If that happens, take a moment to sit with that feeling, and then remember that being liked is not your job. In the best dynamics, the person with a typical amount of charisma can leverage the good vibes created by their high-powered teammate, rather than be overshadowed by them.

I interviewed a junior employee at a company who seemed anxious and uncertain at the outset. My objective was to learn about their work processes, but when introducing themselves (over Zoom) they mentioned there were rabbits in the room with them. Before going into my prepared questions about work processes, I asked about their rabbits. It reduced the intensity of the situation and allowed them to talk about themselves and share something they were comfortable with. I took my cue from them and deviated from my plan in order to help establish rapport.

NOTE HOW DO YOU DO, FELLOW KIDS?

> I interviewed a college-aged man in the home he shared with roommates. He took my questions seriously and did his best to think about what he was being asked before answering. I was accompanied by my client, a confident professional who gave off a friendly "bro" energy. Whenever my client asked a question, our participant's face just lit up with enthusiasm; he smiled, and nodded, and his speech got a little more slang in it. At first, I felt a bit marginalized, as the older uncool guy in the room, but eventually I got over myself and saw how this was a good thing for the interview. I began giving my client more space to ask questions and then moving to follow up myself.

In an interview with a successful neurosurgeon, when I asked them to introduce themself, they pointed to the copies of their published books on their office bookshelves and a framed photograph of their Ivy-educated adult child throwing out the first pitch at a major league baseball game. They had very strong opinions about the design concepts we were showing them, and eventually they grew impatient with me reading out the carefully crafted captions for each image I showed them, and insisted on looking through the pages on their own. When we left the interview, my client expressed sympathy over the rude treatment. I am hardly the model of self-actualized immunity to how I'm treated by others, but rather than being hurt by this interaction, I was very enthusiastic. This interview was great! The stuff they gave me was gold!

The interviewee didn't treat me with respect, and didn't seem to like me, and I don't think I liked them, but we established a dynamic together where I learned interesting and valuable information and experienced no harm. Their (potentially interpreted as arrogant) presentation about their accomplishments, for example, was in response to *my* question, and seemed extremely authentic to who this person was. Their impatience with my process for leading the interview took away my agency, but their opinions and criticisms were very specific and very insightful about the decisions my client's team was facing. Rapport, here, was not about making a best friend, but about establishing an interpersonal dynamic where I was getting the information

I came for. I'll reiterate that I did not experience harm from this interview, but that was me, and that was this single instance.

As in life, you'll meet some people who you'll connect with easily and others who you'll have to work hard to establish that rapport. Bring that awareness with you, and don't set unrealistic expectations for yourself.

DEALING WITH DISRESPECTFUL RESEARCH PARTICIPANTS

By Gregg Bernstein

Gregg Bernstein is a user research leader and author of Research Practice.[2] *An earlier version was published at* https://gregg.io/dealing-with-aggressive-participants

Engaging with research participants is typically a rewarding experience. We meet and learn from new and interesting people, we listen intently, and we probe to uncover motivations and sentiment. Depending on the subject matter, we might encounter raw nerves and strongly expressed feelings. This is all par for the course and within the bounds of expected participant behavior.

I start every interview by encouraging my participants to express their honest feedback, and I explain that what they share won't hurt my feelings. After all, if I interview someone who feels anger about recent changes to a product because it impacted their productivity, they are well within their rights to complain and use colorful language. Their attitude is completely understandable and offers me a great opportunity to demonstrate empathy.

However, as with all things research, there's nuance and subjectivity to unpack: how do we draw boundaries between strongly expressed feelings and aggressive behavior? Between colorful language and offensive speech? As researchers, we strive to create a safe space for our participants to express themselves, but we must also foster an environment in which we ourselves feel safe.

continues

---

2   Gregg Bernstein, *Research Practice: Perspectives from UX Researchers in a Changing Field* (North Charleston, SC: Greggcorp, LLC, 2021), https://gregg.io/book

When a participant directed sexist language at a member of my research team, she opted to immediately and prematurely end the session. This was the right course of action, and I made it clear to my team that we're all empowered to make such decisions.

To limit such behavior from future participants, my team and I drafted an updated consent form that prohibits the use of racist or misogynistic language, hate speech, or personal attacks. In the interest of creating a safe environment, this new form applies to both participants and researchers. As with any binding agreements between your organization and your participants, be sure to run any changes by your legal team. After I consulted my organization's legal team, we updated our consent form with this language:

> [Organization] expects that researchers and participants will be respectful and professional to one another. Discriminatory language, harassment, or hate speech will not be tolerated. Any party may end the research session at any time, for any reason.

The consent form offers one layer of protection. If a participant ventures into personal attacks or prohibited language, you should take further steps to protect yourself. If you're conducting remote research, end the call and email the participant a copy of their signed consent with a note that states that you terminated the session due to their violation of the agreed upon terms. If you're conducting research in a facility, have the participant removed from the premises. If you're doing research on-site, leave. Work with your organization's security team to develop a plan that is specific to your context.

As researchers, we position ourselves as an interface between our organizations and our users. We encounter a spectrum of emotions delivered at various intensities. In this role, we have to be ever mindful of differentiating feedback directed *to* us from language directed *at* us. Hopefully, it never becomes an issue, but plan now for how you and your team will manage disrespectful research participants.

Be Selective About Social Graces

Your participants have no framework for an "ethnographic interview," so they will likely be mapping this experience onto something more familiar like "having company" (when being interviewed at home) or "taking a meeting" or "giving a demo" (when being interviewed about their work). Sometimes when you visit people in their homes, they will offer you a drink. For years, I resisted taking the drink, trying to minimize the inconvenience I was causing. I was well intentioned but naïve; one time I declined a proffered drink and met an ongoing undercurrent of hostility. They made the drink offer a second time, maybe with a bit of expectation, so I accepted, and suddenly everything thawed. The issue wasn't my pursuit or denial of refreshment, it was acknowledging my participant's social expectations—guests should act like guests. This experience took place in the U.S. In other parts of the world (say, Japan), these rituals are even more inflexible and failure to adhere to them will likely doom the interview. Be sure that you're aware of the social expectations in the culture in which you conduct your interviews.

Small talk is a common technique for building rapport. It's not just irrelevant chatter—it plays an important role in how you connect with and feel safe interacting with other people, provides an underlying structure to guide conversation, and transitions into and out of different modes of conversation[3] (see Chapter 4, "The Successful Fieldwork Experience"). You might talk about an item in the room, or the weather, or whether or not to take off your shoes. Find a balance between too little small talk (which can feel abrupt and even rude) and too much small talk (which can create confusion about what this session is going to be and when it's going to start).

NOTE SMALL TALK, BIG WHOOPS

In remote video interviews, small talk serves an essential function as interviewer and participant try to come together into a common (virtual) space. You might ask about where they are geographically located (as it's not uncommon not to have that information before the interview starts) and what the weather is like. You might ask about a nature panorama they've featured in their virtual background. When the physical experience isn't shared, it is worth the effort to share the virtual space.

---

3 Justine Coupland, "Small Talk: Social Functions," *Research on Language & Social Interaction* 36, no. 1 (2003): 1–6, https://doi.org/10.1207/S15327973RLSI3601_1

At the beginning of a session, I said to one of the participants "Can I ask about your background?" by which I meant a really unique and vibrant image behind them, virtually. They responded with a detailed description of their professional trajectory, the logical interpretation of my accidentally ambiguous question. I was trying to make small talk, and I would have never asked for their career arc so early and aggressively. It reminded me that how we communicate virtually requires an additional step to establish a shared context.

Be Selective When Talking About Yourself

You are bound to hear stories in the field that you strongly identify with, whether it's someone's frustration with finding an EV charging station or how much they love reading autobiographical fiction. Although it's important to connect with your participant, it's not the best idea to get there by sharing your common interest. Remember that the interview isn't about you. If you also love autobiographical fiction, you may think "OMG! Another fellow autofiction enthusiast! I wonder if they read Karl Ove Knausgaard?" *But you don't have to say that!* Think about when to reveal something about yourself (and when not to). Putting a "me too!" out there changes the dynamic of the interview.

The naïve interviewer assumes they will connect with their participant by sharing about themselves. Although this approach might work in social settings, where "see how much we have in common!" is a way we establish our worth, it can be detrimental in an interview. It takes the focus away from them and puts it onto you. You can be interested in their challenges in charging their EV without bringing your experience into the interview at all. When I asked the participant about their rabbits (earlier in the chapter), I didn't talk about my pets. I kept the focus on them.

I interviewed stakeholders on-site at a Silicon Valley company. One of the people I met was visiting from the Vancouver office, and just days before I had been visiting my family who live in Vancouver. I enthusiastically mentioned this at the outset of our meeting and was met with an entirely disinterested reaction. We had a good interview, but later I wondered "Wow, what was their problem?" I ruminated about it for a day or so until I heard myself and what I was saying! I had asked for this person's time, and I started off talking about myself and expected that they would be interested?

Sometime after that, working with a different American company, I met with a Canadian team member who vented some of his long-standing gripes over being disregarded by his American counterparts (and Americans in general), wearily joking that "you spell 'check' wrong! It's c-h-e-q-u-e not c-h-e-c-k." As someone who immigrated to the U.S. from Canada, his riffing (which was presented with humor but exposed real frustration) brought up a lot of feelings for me. I kept quiet. I felt a lot of "I knowwwwwwwww!" bubbling inside of me, trying to get out, but to say anything would only have served me and not the interview.

In an in-home interview to talk about music, I was seated with a partial view of a poster of Mick Jagger. Over the course of the interview, the participant shared wonderful stories about the music they liked (local rappers from their current city and their original hometown). As the interview wrapped up, I asked about their poster of Mick Jagger, but as we stood up, they looked confused and showed me that it was actually a poster of Bob Marley. It *did* look like Mick from where I was sitting, but I didn't need to say anything. I felt hopeful that after hearing about music I didn't relate to that I could make a connection over a performer that *I* liked. In the alternative history version of this story, I stand up and say "Bob Marley! Cool poster!" and the participant tells me "Yeah, I bought that poster in Atlanta," and we wrap things up on a positive note. My intention here came from a moment of insecurity and played out awkwardly. These authentic, if incidental, moments are important. It's best to be aware of your intention so you can choose the appropriate moment to express yourself authentically.

You should definitely talk about yourself if doing so gives your participant permission to share something. I interviewed an outgoing person who worked in a somewhat obscure role that my partner also works in. When our participant described their work, I didn't say anything. Much later in the interview, they became hesitant as they began explaining how, as compassionate as they clearly were, sometimes they would relieve stress with morbid humor. At that point, I referenced my partner and that I had seen similar behavior from her and her colleagues. This small and well-timed revelation normalized what the interviewee was sharing and helped us move forward with the interview.

As we rang the doorbell, my colleague and I unconsciously straightened, preparing ourselves for that all-important first impression, that moment when our research participant would come to the door and size us up. We waited for a moment, looking at each other as we heard footsteps, mustering a smile as the inside door opened.

"Hello," I offered. "Are you Brian?"

As I began to state the obvious, that we were here for the interview, he grunted, opened the screen door, and as we took hold, he turned around and walked back into the house. We glanced at each other and stepped into the foyer. What did we know about Brian? Our recruiting screener told us he was 22, lived with his parents and brother, and was employed part-time. The rest would be up to us to discover.

It was 7:30 in the morning, and we were taking our shoes off in a strange house. Eventually, someone beckoned from the kitchen, and we went in. But already we were out of sync. The kitchen was small, with an L-shaped counter and a small table for dining. Brian's mother was at the end of the L, working with bowls and dishes and burners on the stove. Brian's father was perched against the counter, while Brian and his younger brother sat at the table. His father was a small man, while the other three were quite large. The room wasn't big enough for the six of us, so we managed to set up for the interview in the only place we could—at the far end of the counter. We wedged ourselves (one behind the other) on small chairs, pulling our knees in, our paraphernalia of notepads, documents, video cameras, tapes, batteries, and so on clutched in close. It wasn't ideal, but we hoped we could make it work.

The real challenge became clear quickly. Although Brian had agreed to be interviewed, he was actively disinterested. We had recruited Brian specifically, but here we were with the entire family. We pressed ahead, explaining our study, and starting in with our planned questions. Since Brian was the person with whom we had the arrangement, we focused our attention on him. He responded with one-word answers (which sounded more like grunts) and the occasional glance at his brother, causing them both to giggle.

My colleague and I avoided looking at each other (it may not have been physically possible, given the tight quarters) for fear of displaying our despair. Sure, we had arranged this interview, but the cues we were receiving were making it clear the arrangement wasn't worth much. At this point, we had already awoken quite early to conduct this interview, so there was no point in giving up. If they changed their mind explicitly, they'd let us know, and we'd leave. Meanwhile, what else was there to do but press on? I asked questions with very little response. I tried the brother, at which point Brian bolted out of the room for a few minutes, without a word. The brother was only slightly more amenable than Brian, mostly interested in making critical comments about his parents (to Brian's great grunting enjoyment), rather than providing any actual information.

It appeared that Brian had not informed his parents that we were coming. Although I directed some of the questioning toward his mom, she reacted with pretty serious hostility, informing us (in the context of an answer to a question) that they did not welcome strangers into their house, and (while she was preparing food) highlighted the intimate nature of food preparation as a symbol, which was even less open to strangers. The message was very clear.

But again, what could we do? Pressing on until we were specifically asked to leave, under the explicit agreement we had made, seemed the best approach. We asked our questions, following up on the information they had shared, listening closely, looking for clarification, offering up as much space as we could for them to talk, all in trying to build some flow and dialogue.

Even though the message was negative, at least the parents were willing to talk to us. And so, the young men faded out of the conversation, and the interview eventually switched over to the parents. Two hours later, it turned out that we had completed an excellent interview with them; they each had great stories about our topic area and revealed a lot of background about their family, about growing up, about their activities, and even their perspectives on what made the United States the country it had become. By not giving up, by ignoring our own discomfort, and by being patient in building rapport, a near-failure turned into a triumph.

Before we left the house, the mother insisted on cooking up some fried bread, fresh and hot for us. She stated that "No one comes here and doesn't get food," thus reiterating the intimate nature of food she had mentioned at the beginning, but this time as a compliment rather than a warning.

continues

As soon as we left the house, my colleague turned to me and said, "I don't know how you pulled that off; I thought we were done for and would have to leave." I was very pleased with how the interview turned out, especially because it began so poorly, but there was little magic to it. I didn't try to solve the big problem of the complex dynamic we had walked into; I just focused (especially at first) on the next problem—the immediate challenge of what to say next. I was certainly keeping the larger goals in mind of how to cover all the areas we were interested in, but I was focusing my energy as an interviewer on the next point. And by working at it in small pieces, bit by bit, the dynamic shifted. As interviewers, we had to compartmentalize the social experience of the event—the extreme discomfort and awkwardness of the early part of the interview—and stick to our jobs. We didn't handle the situation that differently than any other interview, and it served as a testament to our approach—listening, following up (and showing that we were listening by the way we followed up), building rapport and trust bit by bit, until there was a great deal of openness and great information.

There are better ways to communicate with the participants ahead of time to screen out the unwilling. I should have spoken directly to the person we were visiting before the day of the interview, in order to get that person-to-person communication started early. But there's still a good chance that you'll end up with someone sometime who isn't initially comfortable with the interview process, and it's your job to make them comfortable. Doing so may make you uncomfortable, but with practice, you'll learn to set aside social dynamics and focus on the question asking and listening that will make the interview a success. Some of your best interviews may be with people who are visibly uncomfortable or disinterested at the outset. See Chapter 7, "Better Interviews," for more on troubleshooting common interview problems.

The Interview Is an Atypical Event

Although your participants are using "social call" or "vendor meeting" as their initial framework for their experience with you, it's not a perfect model. Strangers don't typically visit you and take videos of you grinding coffee beans. Falling back on naturalistic observation is disingenuous; it's not easy for participants to pretend you aren't there and just go on as they would normally. If you make the generous assumption that people on reality TV shows are in fact behaving naturally, that is typically due to an extensive amount of time surrounded by cameras, where what is *natural* shifts to something different. You won't have enough time in your interview to accomplish that. Instead, leverage the constructed nature of your shared experience. You are empowered to ask silly-seeming detailed questions about the mundane because you are joined together in this uncommon interaction. Frame some of your questions with phrases such as "What I want to learn today is…" as an explicit reminder that you have different roles in this shared, unnatural experience.

Listen

When you engage in conversation, you're often thinking about what you want to say next and listening for the breathing cues that indicate it's your turn to speak. As you jockey for your 51 percent of the conversation space, listening becomes a limited resource. Although we all like to consider ourselves "good listeners," for interviewing, you must rely on a very special form of listening that goes beyond the fundamentals, such as "don't interrupt."

Listening is the most effective way you can build rapport.[4] It's how you demonstrate tangibly to your participants that what they have to say is important to you.

---

4   Research that analyzed getting-to-know-you conversations in both social and speed-dating found that "people who ask more questions, particularly follow-up questions…are perceived as higher in…listening, understanding, validation, and care." K. Huang, M. Yeomans, A. W. Brooks, J. Minson, and F. Gino, "It Doesn't Hurt to Ask: Question-Asking Increases Liking," *Journal of Personality and Social Psychology* 113, no. 3 (2017): 430–452, https://doi.org/10.1037/pspi0000097

Listen by Asking Questions

In addition to demonstrating listening by what you *don't* say, you can also demonstrate that you are listening by what you *do* say. Most of the questions you actually ask, and the way you ask them, should be emergent—they should come from what the person has said. The questions you ask are indicators that you are listening. Try to construct each question as a follow-up to a previous answer. You'll need to follow up to get clarity and additional detail until you get to the point where you understand what they are trying to tell you. When you go back to something from before, tell them "I want to go back to something you said before." When you change topics, just tell them that you're changing topics with a phrase like "Okay, I'm going to switch gears here and maybe we can talk about planning out budgets now." This approach reinforces that you are paying attention to what they are telling you, it's important information, and you want to know more about it—or that you are partnering with them in this conversation, and you are making sure they're tracking with you where it's headed. This really increases rapport.

Be Aware of Your Body Language

Use your eyes to signal your commitment to the interview. Some amount of eye contact is good, but also aim your gaze at their face, their hands, and items they are showing you. Acknowledge their comments with gentle head nods (you can even just duck your chin down rather than a full up-and-down bob) or simple "mm-hmm" sounds. Be conscious of your body position. When you are listening, you should be leaning forward and visibly engaged (see Figure 5.7). When you aren't listening, your body tells that story, too (see Figure 5.8).

Sometimes advice about body language gets oversimplified into "Don't cross your arms! It creates a barrier." Again, intent wins the day. You can experiment with different poses: arms crossed, but interested and open versus arms crossed and disinterested. Notice how your mindset shows up differently, even with the supposedly negative folded arms.

If your brain is listening, your body will naturally follow. But there's growing evidence that it works the other way, too! Just as therapists and life coaches encourage people to "act as if," you can also put your body into a listening posture and your brain will follow. Consider the example described by Malcolm Gladwell in his article "The

Naked Face."[5] A group of psychologists were developing a coding system for facial expressions. As they identified the muscle groups and what different combinations signified, they realized that in moving those muscles, they themselves were experiencing those feelings. He writes: "Emotion doesn't just go from the inside out. It goes from the outside in... In the facial-feedback system,[6] an expression you do not even know that you have can create an emotion you did not choose to feel."

FIGURE 5.7
Engaged body language puts the speaker into listening mode and communicates their intent to the person they are speaking with.

FIGURE 5.8
Disengaged body language like this sends a negative message to the person you are speaking with.

---

5   Malcolm Gladwell, "The Naked Face," *The New Yorker,* August 5, 2002, www.newyorker.com/magazine/2002/08/05/the-naked-face

6   Later work about the facial feedback hypothesis demonstrated the connection between our body and our internal state. Laura Castañón, "Global Collaboration Led by Stanford Researcher Shows That a Posed Smile Can Improve Your Mood," *Stanford News,* October 20, 2022, https://news.stanford.edu/2022/10/20/posing-smiles-can-brighten-mood/

Optimizing for Remote

In 2020, many of us began spending a vastly increased amount of time on Zoom and other video chat platforms. The term from that time—"Zoom fatigue"—refers to the toll of talking to people over video. Professor Jeremy Bailenson of the Stanford Virtual Human Interaction Lab identified key causes of Zoom fatigue and suggested some work-arounds.[7]

For example:

- Looking at large faces is unnatural, so take your video chat out of full screen and reduce the size of the window.

- Seeing your own image is taxing and invites you to be critical of yourself, so turn off self-view.

- The cognitive load is higher over video than in other regular face-to-face communication, so take breaks from both being on video yourself and from looking at others on video.

Eye Contact

Making eye contact—a signal that you are listening—is harder over video chat. Your natural instinct is to look at someone's eyes, or at least their face. But the camera is on the monitor bezel, so looking at their face means that you aren't looking at the camera, and thus aren't making the ideal eye contact. One whimsical work-around is to simulate a face near the camera lens, with googly eyes or a sticky note. You're still looking away from the face, which takes an effort, but perhaps it's easier than staring at the lens.

I also try to arrange the windows on my computer screen so that the other person's face is as close as possible to the top of the monitor. Some video chat programs make that very difficult by putting controls and other information above the incoming video. Still, the closer you get, the less dramatic your off-angle eye contact will be.

Depending on what you are doing to run a research session remotely, you may be making notes in a different window, or writing by hand, or operating a slide presentation, etc., so you might want to call attention to the dynamics at the beginning of the interview, telling your

---

7 Vignesh Ramachandran, "Stanford Researchers Identify Four Causes for 'Zoom Fatigue' and Their Simple Fixes," *Stanford News*, February 23, 2021, https://news.stanford.edu/2021/02/23/four-causes-zoom-fatigue-solutions/

participant "I'm going to be writing by hand while we talk, so you may notice me not looking directly at you, but of course I'm listening!" Calling this out will help the two of you create a collaborative context for your virtual interaction.

Other Body Language Cues

Over a video connection, the body language cues you rely on when face-to-face don't come through, or they come through differently. In person, you unconsciously attend to breath sounds that indicate the other person is ready to talk. Video chat typically only delivers the audio for who it considers to be speaking, so pre-interruption noises like inhaling don't come through.

When your normal indicators of "I want to say something" are thwarted, you may be tempted to escalate. (Indeed, video chat platforms include a "raise hand" function for that reason.) These indicators could include: leaning forward with your mouth open, furrowing your brow, rubbing your temples, holding your chin, looking away from the screen while nodding, and so on. And while those are feedback indicators, they are also seeking acknowledgment and asking your participant to make space for you. While the tactics shift, the principles are the same as with in-person interviews: try to be still and listen, minimize your affirmation, and choose the specific moments when you want to be heard. Because video chat changes some of your default behaviors, it's more important than ever to be mindful of your physical presence and the choices you are making.[8]

Turn Off Your Camera

Before videoconferencing became more widely used, researchers often conducted research over the telephone. That's still an option. Or you can use a video chat platform but turn the camera off. You can have the camera on at the beginning of the session for small talk and introductions, and then ask your participant to turn off their camera after that. Terry Gross, the host of NPR's talk show *Fresh Air*, is known for eschewing any visual context at all for her interviews. Similarly, the psychotherapist's traditional couch serves to create

---

8 In this video, Lee the puppet and his friend Mary Robinette Kowal have some tips for how body language in a video window conveys interest, listening, and so on. It's all good, but skip to 6:45 for the most applicable bits, www.youtube.com/watch?v=Qc-m95HRYXM

intimacy specifically by avoiding looking at the other person. There's plenty of precedent to make an explicit choice not to use video for the entirety of your interview.

Managing the Setup

Remote research can use multiple devices, screens, and windows. Your best setup will vary by the equipment you have access to and your own style. Here's one example from Shannon Stoll: She uses a widescreen monitor with the participant's video on one side and the interview guide on the other (Figure 5.9). She's able to lead the interview and pay occasional attention to the observer's chat, so she keeps her notifications turned on (although she calls this "the user research equivalent of texting and driving"). She takes notes on pen and paper, and when she has to break eye contact, she'll tell the participant "I'm just going to write that down, quick."

IMAGE COURTESY OF SHANNON STOLL

FIGURE 5.9
It's important to configure both your virtual and physical desktop so that you can interact with your materials, your participant, and your observers.

The Last Word

Experts have a set of best practices—tactics, really—that they follow. But what really makes them expert is that they have a set of operating principles. This looks more like a framework for how *to be,* rather than a list of what *to do.*

- Check your worldview at the door. When you begin fieldwork, don't fixate on what you expect to learn, but rather cultivate your own general, nonspecific curiosity.

- Embrace how other people see the world. Do your fieldwork in their environments—not in yours. Before you head out to the field, get the team together and do a cleansing brain dump of all the things you might possibly expect to see and hear, leaving you open to what is really waiting for you out there.

- One of the factors that makes for great interviews is the rapport that you establish between you and your participant. Don't forget that it's up to you to build that rapport. Focus on them and be very selective about talking about yourself.

- Your job is to listen, beyond "Keep your mouth shut and your ears open." Your choice of questions and how you ask them is a way to demonstrate that you are listening. Your body language cues your participant—and you—as to how well you are paying attention.

The Intricacies of Asking Questions

So, there you are in "the field," that coolest of phrases that means that today your assignment is to talk with a stranger in their kitchen, maintenance shed, copy center, or another unlikely environment. As you get down to business, your printed copy of the interview guide is gripped tightly in your sweaty paw. All your objective-setting, question-wordsmithing, and other planning is captured in 11-point type on these precious four sheets of paper.

Now, set it aside.

Leading the interview successfully comes down to *you*. Go ahead and refer to the guide as you need to, but don't let it run the interview. It's not a script; it's only for reference purposes. If you get stuck about where to go next, that's when you turn to it and scan through the pages. Despite your planning, the interview probably won't unfold the way you anticipated. If it does, perhaps you aren't leveraging enough of the opportunities that arise. If you're a novice interviewer, you'll probably lean more toward the guide than improvisation. Similarly, if you're at the very beginning of a study, you should rely more on the guide than you will once you've learned from a couple of interviews.

FROM MY PERSPECTIVE

DIFFERENT RESEARCH TOPICS REQUIRE DIFFERENT INTERVIEWING MUSCLES

In some research studies, I led similar interviews that broadly followed the guide's questions and flow. Other research topics required individual, exploratory conversations. In one set of interviews about remote work, I sought to understand how employees were using their home to work. Each session basically followed the interview guide. In another set of interviews with the same population, I was learning about how people managed their relationships while working remotely. For this topic, I had made plenty of assumptions (or hypotheses) about what the issues and questions would be and how to even begin talking about them.

But each interview was an improv exercise to figure out how to explore *this* topic with *this* person. We were sampling the same population with the same general theme and yet the interviews were entirely different. As you go from project to project, even with the same user base, be aware that you will find yourself using different interviewing muscles. ■

There's Power in Your Silence

After you ask a question, be silent. This is tricky because you are speaking with someone you've never spoken to before. You are learning about their conversational rhythm, how receptive they are to your questions, and what cues they give when thinking about an answer. These tiny moments—from part of a second to several seconds—are nerve-wracking.

One way a novice interviewer tries to counteract nervousness is by preemptively filling the silence. So, the interviewer asks long questions. What they want to know is, "What did you have for breakfast yesterday?" but the novice stretches the question out to delay that moment where the question is done, and then is forced to await the answer (or some awful unnamed fate). The question then becomes "What did you have for breakfast yesterday...was it toast or juice?" The novice interviewer is suggesting possible responses, and their interviewee is just that much more likely to work within the interviewer's suggestions rather than offer up their own answers. In fact, what the novice interviewer probably asked was, "What did you have for breakfast yesterday? Was it toast, or juice, or...?" You can hear the novice interviewer actually articulate the ellipsis, as a descending, slowly fading "Rrrrrrrr?" That trailing sound is the last gasp at holding onto the question.

Don't do this. Ask your question and let it stand. Be deliberate about this. To deal with your (potentially agonizing!) discomfort during the silence, give yourself something to do—slowly repeat "allow silence" as many times as it takes. Use this as a mantra to calm and clear your mind (at least for the moment). Or place one finger in front of your lips to communicate focused listening to your participant, which also has the advantage of slightly restricting your mouth from moving (see Figure 6.1).

Rest assured that if your participant can't answer the question, they will let you know. If you pay attention to your participant's body language, you'll see (usually, long before you stop talking) their facial expression indicates when they have something to say. You can optionally do a hard stop at that point, "...oh, go ahead!" to confirm that you're paying attention to them, and that you want to hear what they have to say.

FIGURE 6.1
Placing a finger over your mouth gently restricts your ability to speak, while conveying that you are listening intently.

In the previous bad example, the interviewer, fearing the uncertainty of a short question, and going too far with making the question easier to answer, offered a closed set of choices: toast or juice? Offering a list of options to an otherwise open-ended question is extremely common. Here are two examples.

From the excellent podcast *99 Percent Invisible:*[1]

> **Tom Geismar:** And we often have a favorite, which we try to push if we have. But there's not necessarily the obvious right answer.
>
> **Roman Mars:** And when you have a favorite, do you plainly state that it's your favorite or do you just present it first or present it last? Is there a gamesmanship in this at all?

From an article in the *New Yorker*[2] by Joshua Rothman:

> "Now that you're getting closer to putting a device in a person, how does it feel?" I asked. "Is it exciting, or freaky, or what?"

---

1   Roman Mars, "Making a Mark: Visual Identity with Tom Geismar," *99 Percent Invisible* (podcast), February 13, 2018, https://99percentinvisible.org/episode/making-mark-visual-identity-tom-geismar/transcript/

2   Joshua Rothman, "How to Build an Artificial Heart," *The New Yorker*, March 1, 2021, www.newyorker.com/magazine/2021/03/08/how-to-build-an-artificial-heart

When you present your participant with a specific set of options, you turn an open question into a close-ended, multiple-choice question. Even worse, as a multiple-choice question, it's terrible, as you aren't actually expecting the responses will only come from the examples offered (like toast or juice; or exciting or freaky). You might believe that people will simply tell you their answer, regardless of whether or not it's one of those options, like "leftover pizza" or "it's not a big deal." In any interview, for the first couple of times you do this, maybe they will. But the more you ask questions this way, the more your participant will begin to assume that those are your *preferred* responses. As an interviewer, you typically have a lot of power[3] and using close-ended questions demonstrates to your participant how they can do a good job in the interview, something they generally are eager to do. Adding "...or what" to the end of your options doesn't do much to mitigate the list of options you've already provided. It's better to just ask what you want to know: "What did you have for breakfast?" or "How do you handle it with your client when you have a favorite?" or "Now that you're getting closer to putting a device in a person, how does it feel?"

On the rare occasions when someone struggles with your question (for example, responding with "So... do you mean *everything* about that platform or just about how the platform is used by the moderators?"), try to see that as a good thing! It might feel like you failed with a poorly articulated question, but your participant is demonstrating the rapport they have with you and working with you to make sure that they are helping you get the information you need.

Finally, let's go back to that question about your participant's breakfast. After they have given you an initial answer, continue to be silent. People speak in paragraphs, and they want your permission to go on to the next paragraph. You've asked, "What did you have for breakfast yesterday?" There's a second of silence, and they told you, "I had toast and a bit of yogurt, and then about 20 minutes later I had steak and eggs."

The novice interviewer figures it's time to move on to the next question and asks "Oh, okay. Where did you buy those groceries?" But the best play is just to rest for another beat. Usually, the person will

---

3 A recurring feature on the HBO show *Last Week Tonight with John Oliver* was "'60 Minutes' Anchors Prompting Interviewees to Give the Exact Soundbite They Need," which demonstrates this point to comic effect. One example is www.youtube.com/watch?v=jMOlrkdr7lo

continue. "Well, in fact, yesterday was quite unusual because what I typically do is just have a granola bar, but my sister was coming to visit, and I had to prepare for all of us before she got here." By simply not asking your next question immediately, you give your interviewee time to flesh out the answer they've already given you. Try to develop a sense for when the thread is played out, and it's time for your next question.

> **NOTE** SHUT UP/SHUTTIN' UP
>
> In *Working: Researching, Interviewing*, Writing, Robert Caro writes about the use of silence in interviewing.[4] He mentions "fiction's greatest interviewers"—Inspector Maigret and George Smiley, and their tactics to "keep themselves from talking and let silence do its work." Maigret fiddles with his pipe and Smiley uses his tie to polish his glasses. Caro has his own brilliant technique: "When I'm waiting for the person I'm interviewing to break a silence by giving me a piece of information I want, I write 'SU' (for Shut Up!) in my notebook. If anyone were ever to look through my notebooks, he would find a lot of 'SUs.'"

The Backchannel Trap

In linguistics, a *backchannel* response is a verbal or nonverbal interjection (something nonsubstantive, in contrast to an interruption, which is more substantial) that communicates that the listener understands, is paying attention, or agrees with what the first speaker is saying.

This is a natural part of conversation. It's natural to want to behave encouragingly toward your participant, perhaps out of empathy, or perhaps because you yourself are feeling uncertain.

The typical verbal interjections are familiar: right, uh-huh, okay, sure, yes, got it. A typical nonverbal interjection is nodding. But when your backchannel response signals affirmation or validation (Wow! Uh-huh, Yeah, yeah, Cool, cool, Of course) instead of an acknowledgment (Ah, Mmm, Oh), you're impacting the information you are getting. By telling your participant how you feel about what they are sharing, you influence them to gain more approval.

---

4   Robert Caro, *Working: Researching, Interviewing, Writing* (New York: Alfred A. Knopf, 2019).

This dynamic is a theme we'll return to, and it plays out in this fundamental interaction. All you're trying to do is give permission for your participant to continue to the next paragraph. Try to offer the minimal response. You can turn "mm-hmm" into "mm" or even "m" (more of a soft grunt). Your emphatic head-nod can be just dipping your chin, once, or even widening your eyes and raising your head slightly. The thing to practice is displaying "I heard you" with the minimum amount of vocalization and movement.

This gesture could be challenging at first, but you may find it surprising how this posture gives you focus and confidence. And what you're trying to move away from is the novice interview who is brimming over with enthusiasm and saying "Cool! Cool, cool!" just before their participant has finished the last syllable of their sentence.

NOTE PRESENT AND ACCOUNTED FOR

My advice for interviewers to limit their emotional reactions can cause concern when considering situations when participants share something emotional. You don't want to come off as cold or unkind. But the default "Ohh, I'm sorry!" response can be based on our preemptive assumption about what another person needs from us. As an interviewer, you can treat something vulnerable or difficult they've shared as precious by staying present with them. You can demonstrate your compassion by asking a follow-up question, or remaining very still, or leaning forward, or holding eye contact, or releasing eye contact, or leaving space before your next question. You don't necessarily need to say anything in direct response, especially before knowing their own feelings about what they've experienced. Expressions of sympathy are much more about the person offering them. The choices you make should center your participant.

NOTE THE MINIMUM VIABLE RESPONSE

Since videoconferencing makes it harder to interject, and provides fewer body language cues, we tend to overcompensate with our gestures,[5] like nodding with exaggerated depth and frequency. If you're trying to reduce your backchannel over remote, be mindful of how you've adapted your everyday body language in video meetings. Just like the previous in-person guidance, experiment with the minimum response, although it may be harder (and less desirable) for you to hold back to the same extent.

NOTE PARAGRAPH SPEAK

People do speak in paragraphs. You can see evidence of this by looking at an interview transcription. The pauses between blocks of content are interpreted by the transcriptionist as paragraphs.

Werner Herzog's documentary *Grizzly Man* tells the story of Timothy Treadwell, a self-professed naturalist who lived in the wilderness to be close to his beloved grizzly bears, only to be mauled to death. There's a scene in which Franc Fallico, Alaska's state medical examiner, presents a watch, still in an evidence bag, to Treadwell's ex-girlfriend, Jewel Palovak. Herzog, holding the camera, cuts between passively observing the dialogue between the two of them and inserting his own questions about her memory of Treadwell (and his girlfriend who died with him). Finally, Fallico has Jewel sign some official papers, and the process is complete. Herzog doesn't cut and continues to film the two. But nothing is happening! They have uttered their concluding words and smile awkwardly and stare at nothing. Moments tick by and still no cutting. Then Jewel gives a sharp intake of breath, and Herzog, holding the camera, steps forward. Another moment goes by, and she sobs, breaking down for the first time in this entire sequence. "It's the last thing that's left." Herzog is directing the scene while observing and interviewing. He lets a delicate moment hang uncomfortably, and a devastating emotion emerges. That's the power of silence.

---

5   Jeremy N. Bailenson, "Nonverbal Overload: A Theoretical Argument for the Causes of Zoom Fatigue," *Technology, Mind, and Behavior* 2, no. 1 (2021), https://doi.org/10.1037/tmb0000030

By Lynn Shade

Lynn Shade is a freelance UX designer and researcher who previously worked at Claris, Apple, and Adobe. She grew up in Japan and is bilingual.

Most of the user research I've done has been in Asia, Japan for the most part, where I grew up and where global tech companies often request research to understand market needs. But years ago, when working for Apple I accompanied a Dutch colleague, Anke de Jong, to New York for field research of new laptop models. Trained as an industrial designer, Anke designed at the intersection of hardware and software. This made her research interesting in itself, but what I remember most vividly from that trip was being occasionally astonished at her use of silence to impel further comment.

In New York for the most part this technique wasn't necessary since these participants were more than happy to speak. The willingness and eagerness of American study participants to express themselves verbally was the source of considerable discussion among myself and Japanese research colleagues and indirectly caused a problem for us. Silicon Valley management expected interview techniques that worked well in the West, such as asking the participant to speak their thoughts aloud while using the product or quick interviews diving into a focused topic, could be used to quickly and inexpensively confirm U.S. results in other countries. These and other methods that relied on the participant talking tended not to work in Japan. The silent-ish Japanese participant is all too common, and Japanese colleagues and I would discuss and even devote entire conference presentations to how to draw out our quiet participants, what magic combination of factors might encourage them to speak, even, for one research lab, studying what type of microphones worked best to pick up the quiet speech when they did.

However, even New Yorkers can occasionally fall silent after answering a question. At these points, Anke would deliberately not comment or help the user along, waiting calmly. This seemed to me to be putting stress on the interviewee. I'd grow anxious as the silence hung in the air for what seemed like too long. Invariably the interviewee would break it. The further information was often valuable; they'd clarify or amend, or start a new topic with a new observation, or make a connection that offered interesting insights. The interviewees seemed not to mind and often became very talkative.

continues

Using silence as a mechanism to elicit participants to talk wasn't unique as it's a common technique in friendly and otherwise interviews, but it stuck in my head and over the years as I continued doing research in Japan and other parts of Asia I thought quite a bit about that New York experience and silence in general. Silence in user research in Japan is so important. We allowed lots and lots of room for it. There have been entire books written on Japanese silence, but here I'll summarize Japanese conversational silence into three broad categories: silence to set the stage, silence as encouragement, and danger zone silence.

- **Silence to set the stage:** Along with body language, setting-the-stage silence is a bit of silence from both sides to indicate readiness for a shared experience. Both parties take time to set the mood and air for a productive conversation, and some of this work is done with silence. This type of silence takes place here and there during initial greetings and during the interview as topics change but is most obvious when greetings wind down right before initiating the topic at hand. Lest this paint a picture of solemn meditation-like stillness with a temple bell tolling in the background let me hasten to add that those setting-the-stage silences can be quick and casual or longer, depending on personalities. Fairly typical is saying the equivalent of "um" with a trailing silence and the other party nodding, again followed by a bit of silence. Setting-the-stage silence is created partly because silence is considered a more deeply shared experience than talking—a version of that exists in many cultures—and partly showing mutual respect and mutual humility for the other's expertise. The interviewer's task here and during the interview is to match the interviewee's natural response and thought pace, allowing time for both sides to ponder questions.

- **Silence as encouragement:** During the interview, silence indicates making an effort to help the cause along. The interviewee will be silent to show they're thinking the topic over carefully and showing a desire to contribute to the interviewer's goal. The interviewer will be silent to show they're thinking the subject's response over carefully and showing respect for the effort the interviewee made in answering. Frequently, all parties will be silent when faced with a very difficult or complex question to give the topic due diligence and the time it deserves. Essentially, conversational encouragement is created through lots of silence.

- **Danger zone silence:** The tones of silence to watch for are silence indicating resistance and silence indicating confusion. If the Japanese interviewee doesn't feel qualified to answer the question or is confused by a question and unsure, they'll fall silent. This danger zone silence has its own tiny cues and must be broken by interjections from the interviewer. The stuck interviewee is unlikely to break the silence by just starting to talk about something. If this type of silence is prolonged, the interviewee will start experiencing the stress and worry of letting the situation down. Danger zone silence can be avoided altogether by building a thread of trust by setting context and connection from the first contact during the recruitment process and continuing to set context through the interview itself.

The designer Kenya Hara has a rather lovely section in his book *White* on the meaning of emptiness in the Shinto shrine architecture. He describes how the space created by tying the tops of four pillars with ropes creates "emptiness" that has potential as a vessel to receive thoughts and feelings. He later goes on to tie silence to emptiness and suggests that silence has the possibility to enrich mutual comprehension. Building on this, it's hard to imagine silence in Japanese conversation as being created simply to facilitate a means to a certain end. Rather, successful Japanese silence is a friendly empty space that, when created by both parties, exists to allow communication.

Even if you don't feel nervous, you can't really know what's going to happen as you ask a question.[6] Perhaps your participant will start to answer the question while you are asking it. (Indeed, you can see this sometimes when the participant's whole affect changes as they begin to understand the question and their face shifts dramatically as they bring their answer out to the launch pad.) Perhaps they'll be supremely fast-talking[7] and whip out an answer the very moment you've finished asking it. Perhaps they will wait for you to finish your question and take some amount of time to start speaking, and during that gulf between question and answer they may give you really great "I'm thinking" cues (hand rubs chin, eyes gaze away, lips pursed, and so on). Perhaps they'll give you a juicy verbal cue, like "That's a great question...ummmm...." Or they may simply stare at you, giving no quarter, until they answer. Be prepared for any of these!

When we're not in person and technology introduces a very small delay in conversation, we get messed up pretty quickly. The pauses we listen for at the end of someone's speech are not quite in real time, so we start to speak at the same time as the person on the other end of the call. We hear each other start, so we abruptly stop and defer to them. It's challenging to correct this out-of-phase state. Of course, this happens in person as well, without any technologically introduced delay. Some people just have different natural rhythms.

With some participants, it takes me most of the interview to align my pacing with theirs. There's no magic fix, any more than there's an easy way to successfully talk on the phone when you hear an echo of your own voice. This is stuff happening way below conscious thought, down at the autonomic level. At the very least, be mindful of the out-of-sync phenomenon and try to slow...yourself...down.

---

6   Detailed analysis of "turn taking" is part of conversation analysis, a subdiscipline of linguistics. Experts explore how intonation, pausing, and body language inform the interaction between speakers. Unlike your work as an interviewer, conversation analysts don't do their work in real time.

7   A wonderful example is the rapid-fire and overlapping dialogue between Hildy and Burns in the 1940 Howard Hawks film, *His Girl Friday*.

THEY BLINDED ME WITH SILENCE

Many years ago, I was in my first public improv show. We were all amateurs, some with considerable experience, others (like me) essentially beginners. In this performance, we started each scene with one idea (often from the audience) and proceeded with some sort of structure. What often happened was a scramble to move the idea forward—everyone speaking at once, with too many ideas "thrown" in the first few moments to ever solidify into a great scene. Have you ever seen 8-year-olds play soccer? The ball and both teams are a whirling cloud that moves up and down and across the field like the Tasmanian Devil. That was us.

But then the next night I saw the Kids in the Hall—a comedy troupe that has been performing together for a very long time. After the scripted material had finished, the audience was clamoring for more. In advance of the encore, they all walked on stage and thanked us, and then improvised a few jokes before heading off stage to prepare for the encore. All five of them managed to hold the stage coherently. Not everyone spoke at equal length in those few minutes, but at no point did any of them speak on top of one another. It came off as natural and easy, but it was really quite incredible.

Where they succeeded, and we didn't succeed as well (for there are no losers in improv), was in allowing for silence. Each Kid in the Hall was silent for most, if not all, of their unscripted segment. What a powerful contribution they made by not speaking. Isn't that a strange statement to make? A comedy performer contributed by not speaking. How can that be? We tend to expect performance to be the explicit utterances, not the space between them.

There's a lot that can happen without verbalization—posture, gestures, breath sounds, eye gaze, facial reactions, and more. The Kids in the Hall were doing all those the entire time—and they were paying attention to each other. When they were silent, they were actively silent; they were sending and receiving information.

This behavior is crucial when interviewing users. I estimate we speak as little as 20 percent of the time. Yet the interviews are directed and controlled by the interviewer. Nodding, eye contact, and body language all support the participant in providing detailed information.

continues

Of course, there is often more than one researcher on hand. If the first ethnographer remains silent, waiting for the participant to continue, the second interviewer must recognize that, and also listen silently, rather than using the opening as his chance to interview. This collaborative use of silence is something the Kids in the Hall managed, and my improv group did not.

We experience these same challenges in more familiar work settings: brainstorming, meetings, and so on. We work in a society that judges us primarily by our own contributions, rather than the way we allow others to make theirs. If the collaborative silence is not a shared value in a group, there can be a real challenge for those who default to listening, not speaking. We've learned how to give credit to those who utter the pearls, but we don't know how to acknowledge the value of those who choose their moments wisely, who allow others to shine, and who ultimately enable those pearls.

In a 2002 episode of *The Simpsons* (DABF05, "Jaws Wired Shut"), Homer's jaw is wired shut. He is physically unable to speak. He does become a better listener, but most interesting are the positive qualities the people in his life project upon him. Simpsons' Executive Producer Al Jean said: "When Homer gets his jaw wired shut, it makes him into a really decent, wonderful human being." I don't know if Al Jean is getting post-modern on us, but Homer's internal change, through his silence, was fairly minor compared to the differences that other people perceived. For even more on this theme, check out the book *Being There* by Jerzy Kosiński (or the film with Peter Sellers).

How You Ask

The words that make up your question are just part of what you communicate. You are also using *paralinguistic* information (acoustic information like pitch and volume) and *nonlinguistic* information (facial expressions, eye contact, sounds other than words, and body language).

Assuming that you're confined to the printed word here, and that you aren't listening to an audiobook, I can only describe the specifics of how people speak, without being able to actually demonstrate it. But you can do this yourself. Take a simple phrase, like "Honey, I'm home!" and say it out loud. Now, note what happens when you emphasize different words: *Honey,* I'm home vs. Honey, *I'm* home, vs. Honey, I'm *home.* By punching each of those words in turn, you tell a very different story. Next, try saying that phrase with the intention of conveying a different emotion: for example, resigned, tired, enthusiastic, wary, amorous, and angry.[8] Consider how many different ways you can ask the very same question, depending on how you ask and what you're trying to convey.

Develop your own muscles by practicing asking some of your questions aloud and see how you can convey your actual intent through paralinguistic and nonlinguistic cues. For inspiration, listen to this interview between Terry Gross and Brandi Carlisle:[9]

> **Brandi Carlile:** But a lot of it is just based on what I've been told throughout my life and in a way that I felt when I came out of that, which is that I felt a little bit too in tune with how adults feel and how adults walk through the world, as opposed to how a child thinks adults walk through the world.
>
> **Terry Gross:** What do you mean by that?
>
> **Brandi Carlile:** Well, I think that the fallibility that gets exposed when you realize that your parents don't have any control over whether or not you live or die is not something you're supposed to really realize, I think, until you get a lot older...

Gross's clarification question could have come across like a challenge, but in the specific way she says it, I hear her genuine curiosity and gentleness. Be aware of your own potential to really land your question by the way you ask it.

When You Ask

Survey designers consider the "order effects" in writing their questions and the overall flow of the survey. "The order in which questions are asked can influence how people respond; earlier questions can unintentionally provide context for the questions that

---

8 These are both acting exercises, described at Kerry Hishon, "Exercise: Same Lines, Different Meanings," *Theatrefolk* (blog), www.theatrefolk.com/blog/19758-2/

9 "Singer Brandi Carlile Talks Ambition, Avoidance and Finally Finding Her Place," *Fresh Air*, April 5, 2021, https://freshairarchive.org/segments/singer-brandi-carlile-talks-ambition-avoidance-and-finally-finding-her-place. The relevant part starts around 4:10.

follow."[10] In an interview, the question you ask isn't an isolated element, it's part of the larger context of the overall interview, where the rapport builds over time and the participant has more opportunity to reflect. Even if you don't explicitly ask the same question at two different points in the interview, you often will hear preferences or expectations offered at different times.

When you are analyzing the interview, it's worth pondering why you got different answers at different times. To generalize, often the first instance has more to do with presenting the information they assume you'd want to hear, something uncontroversial or even pleasing. People seem more likely to be critical or make requests later on in the interview.

It's possible to seek clarification at this point but you don't want to "catch" your participant being inconsistent and make them feel bad. Before you probe on a changed response with "Earlier you told us...but now you're suggesting that..." be sure that this is a way to get at something new, and that you won't be harmful in doing so.

Navigating the Interview's Path

At a high level, most of the interview can unfold naturally from the kick-off question (see Chapter 4, "The Successful Fieldwork Experience"). Strive to present many of the questions from your interview guide as follow-up questions. Of course, you likely can't do this for the entirety of the interview, but pursuing this ideal will help develop rapport, demonstrate listening, and create an interaction that feels more conversational than interrogatory.

Not everything can be a follow-up. Some threads run out of steam, or sometimes you need to deliberately change the discussion in order to dig into a specific area of interest. The guiding principle here is to *signal your lane changes*. Compare these two snippets of a hypothetical interview:

Version 1

> Q: And what happened when you downloaded the updated version of the iPhone app?
>
> A: (laughs) It installed instantly!
>
> Q: Where do you keep your used oil drums?

---

10 Pew Research Center, "Writing Survey Questions," www.pewresearch.org/
our-methods/u-s-surveys/writing-survey-questions/

Version 2

> Q: And what happened when you downloaded the updated version of the iPhone app?
>
> A: (laughs) It installed instantly!
>
> Q: Okay, this is great. I'm just going to shift direction here. Maybe you can tell us, where do you keep your used oil drums?

In the second snippet, the deliberate, explicit turn signal acknowledges the most recent answer and points the way toward the next, otherwise discontinuous, topic for discussion. As a rule, if your question isn't fairly obviously a follow-up question, you should preface it with some transitional words.

Getting to Even More of the Answer

Here's some bad news: You won't get the answer to your questions just by asking. If only you could simply utter the question and wait while the person gives you all the information you need, and then move on to the next question on your list. That's just not how real interviews go. For most threads, in most interviews, you need to use a series of questions to get to the information you want. It's not that people are being difficult; they just don't know what it is that you want to know. They interpret your question in a certain way and do their best to answer it. But it's up to you to help them tell you what you need to learn.

When you listen to your participant answering your question, be vigilant. Do they appear to have understood what you intended by the question, or have they gone somewhere else with it? Their interpretation may be more revealing than what you intended, so you may just let the conversation go down that path, or you might want to wait for an appropriate time to redirect back to the topic you were initially interested in.

Is there more that you need to probe further on? People sometimes speak in coded terms: " . . . this was before the earlier situation that changed my purchasing . . . ." The "earlier situation" may be something they are uncomfortable revealing, at least for now, or it may be that they aren't sure if they have your permission to share the specifics of the "earlier situation." Even if you don't follow up immediately, it may be a topic you want to return to.

Are you asking the question in a way they can answer? In a study about customer service, a participant complained passionately about the poor telephone service he received from a retailer. I asked him how the service might be different, but he could only speak about the current situation. Eventually, I shifted my tactics entirely, and we role-played an imagined future version of the telephone interactions. My follow-up questions focused on uncovering the specific details that made his scenario a desirable one.

Start with specific questions and follow up with general questions. "How do you typically choose a contractor?" is a hard question to answer as it presumes that the participant has a set of practices in place; if they don't, they may make something up to address your question. Instead, ask about the last time they started a project, and how they chose a contractor, and then ask about whether or not that represents a pattern. It's easier for your participant to give you a more reliable answer that way.

Regardless of how specific your question is, you'll still get general responses. People can be vague because they don't know how much detail you actually care about. Like this example, you can use a follow-up question to get to the specifics.

> **Q:** And so, did you try the Oaxacan food?
>
> **A:** We did, it was great, it was really different.
>
> **Q:** How was it different?

You should be regularly moving between specific and general questions, to get clarity on a particular example and to understand how that example represents their overall approach, mindset, preference, and so on.

A Palette of Question Types

The interview guide is your (highly idealized) hypothesis for how you will ask questions. But really, you'll spend much of your effort in the interview determining the best ways to enable your participant to share with you. Think about your role as trying to lower the barrier and think about questions as the tools you're going to use to do that. So, you need a broad set of question types in order to make this happen. Here are some examples to get you started:

Questions that gather context and collect details:

- **Ask about sequence.** "Describe a typical workday. What do you do when you first sit down at your station? What do you do next?"

- **Ask about quantity.** "How many files would you delete when that happens?"
- **Ask for specific examples.** "What was the last movie you streamed?" Compare that question to "What movies do you stream?" The specific is easier to answer than the general and becomes a platform for follow-up questions.
- **Ask about exceptions.** "Can you tell me about a time when a customer had a problem with an order?"
- **Ask for the complete list.** "What are all the different apps you have installed on your smartphone?" This will require a series of follow-up questions—for example, "What else?" Very few people can generate an entire list of something without some prompting.
- **Ask about relationships.** "How do you work with new vendors?" This general question is especially appropriate when you don't even know enough to ask a specific question (such as in comparison to the earlier example about streaming movies). Better to start general than to be presumptive with a too-specific question.
- **Ask about organizational structure.** "Who do the people in that department report to?"

Questions that probe what's been unsaid:
- **Ask for clarification.** "When you refer to 'that,' you are talking about the newest server, right?"
- **Ask about code words/native language.** "Why do you call it the *bat cave*?"
- **Ask about emotional cues.** "Why do you laugh when you mention Best Buy?"
- **Ask why.** "I've tried to get my boss to adopt this format, but she just won't do it...." "Why do you think she hasn't?"
- **Probe delicately.** "You mentioned a difficult situation that changed your usage. Can you tell me what that situation was?"[11]

---

11 A great example is from the *Bone Valley* podcast, during an interview with someone they believe has committed a murder. The podcast narrator explains "We'd been hoping the taxicab driver would come up in conversation. We didn't want it to feel confrontational. So, when he brings it up, we follow his lead." And then in the interview itself he asks "Can you talk a little bit—you mention the taxi story and I'm just curious, like, how that started. Can you just start that from the beginning?" Gilbert King, "Chapter 9 | Coming Clean," *Bone Valley* (podcast), November 9, 2022, https://lavaforgood.com/podcast/s1e9-chapter-9-coming-clean/

- **Probe without presuming.** "Some people have very negative feelings about the current government, while others don't. What is *your* take?" Rather than the direct "What do you think about our government?" or "Do you like what the government is doing lately?" This indirect approach offers options associated with the generic "some people" rather than the interviewer or the interviewee.
- **Explain to an outsider.** "Let's say that I've just arrived here from another decade, how would you explain to me the difference between smartphones and tablets?"
- **Teach another.** "If you had to ask your daughter to operate your system, how would you explain it to her?"

Questions that create contrasts in order to uncover frameworks and mental models:

- **Ask about both success and failure.** "What's an example of when this went well? What's an example of when it didn't go so well?"
- **Compare processes.** "What's the difference between sending your response by fax, mail, or email?"
- **Compare to others.** "Do the other coaches also do it that way?"
- **Compare across time.** "How have your family photo activities changed in the past five years? How do you think they will be different five years from now?" The second question is not intended to capture an accurate prediction. Rather, the question serves to break free from what exists now and envision possibilities that may emerge down the road. Identify an appropriately large time horizon—(a year, five years, ten years?)—that helps people think beyond incremental change.

Managing the Ebb and Flow of the Interview

As a plan for an idealized interview, the guide is, of course, linear. But the active planning process you go through during the interview is actually more of a tree (see Figure 6.2).

This is a fairly typical snippet of an interview. It's what is going on for the interviewer that deserves some special focus here, though. As the participant is explaining in his natural manner, the interviewer is identifying other questions to ask. At the first pause, the interviewer has at least two new questions (beyond what's already in their interview guide), but the interviewer encourages the participant to continue by responding with "Okay." As the participant continues, they might identify another two topics to be explored. Maybe those topics are included in the interview guide, but probably they aren't.

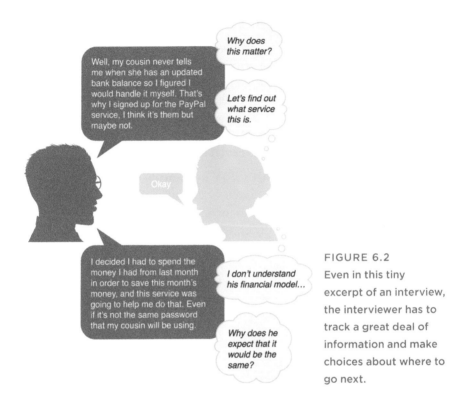

FIGURE 6.2

Even in this tiny excerpt of an interview, the interviewer has to track a great deal of information and make choices about where to go next.

Sadly, most of us are constrained by the linearity of time. We can't clone ourselves and follow each thread in parallel universes. We have to stick with our own reality.

In addition to watching the clock, maintaining eye contact, building rapport, and so on for most of the interview, your job also includes managing this tree. Here are some coping techniques:

1. **Wait patiently** until these threads come up again in conversation organically, without you having to ask. Often, they do.

2. **Jot quick notes** on your interview guide about what you want to come back to, so you don't forget.

3. **Prioritize** based on your research objectives. Although something that seems irrelevant does often prove to be insightful, you have to choose. So be opportunistic and choose what you think is going to bear fruit for your area of inquiry.

4. **Triage** based on what makes the best follow-up, in order to demonstrate listening and further the rapport. Come back to a topic later if it still seems important; refer back to the participant's previous statement in order to establish continuity. ("Earlier you mentioned using PayPal. I wanted to ask a bit more about that.")

I was coaching a group of "people who do research" on interviewing techniques and one person was particularly notable for his easygoing charm. He was very likable, and I sat with him as he led an interview with a customer. This customer explained "I get all these papers together, and then I bring them over to my accountant, and then I go home and have a panic attack!" The interviewer responded, "What do you use to organize those papers?"

I asked the interviewer afterward why he made this choice, and he said that he felt uncomfortable, so he entirely avoided the topic of the customer's emotional reaction. But the customer shared that emotional reaction as a way of testing out whether or not they could trust the interviewer. They made themselves vulnerable, and the interviewer ignored them. This undoubtedly hurt the rapport for the rest of the interview, and it was a missed chance to gather relevant information at that very moment. I still wonder just what it was about this customer's process that led to such a strong reaction!

FROM MY PERSPECTIVE

GOING WITH THE FLOW

The complexity embedded within the exploding questions tree might suggest that interviewing really stinks. In fact, dealing with these challenges can take you to someplace very creative. Mihaly Csíkszentmihalyi has explained the psychological notion of *flow* as "the mental state of operation in which a person in an activity is fully immersed in a feeling of energized focus, full involvement, and success in the process of the activity."[12]

NBA players describe this as "the game slowing down." It certainly happens to me in interviews. My brain is firing on all cylinders with all the responsibilities I'm managing, and yet I can feel myself slow right down. It's a feeling in both my brain and my body, evocative of the familiar special effect, seen through a spaceship's view screen when it enters hyperspace and the stars stretch from points into lines. In this calmness, I'm not ignoring the complexity; instead, I'm somehow above it. Things become very quiet in my head, and I can feel myself riding on top of the challenges

---

12 "Flow (psychology)," Wikipedia, Wikimedia Foundation, https://en.wikipedia
.org/wiki/Flow_(psychology)

of the interview. It's not boredom; it's a very engaged feeling. It's the opposite of the chicken-sans-head feeling you might imagine the demands of an interview could lead to. This flow state both creates and is fed by the imperative to keep silent, keep myself out of the equation, and let the experience breathe, while still being the most creative and insightful time during fieldwork. ■

Embracing Your Participant's Worldview

In Chapter 2, "Research Logistics," I introduced the principle of embracing how participants see their world. That principle informs the entire approach of a study, but it becomes vital once you are with that participant and asking questions. In this section, you'll see how to ensure that your questions make it clear to both you and your participant that you are curious, even hungry, to understand their worldview.

Use Their Language

Years ago, I was working with a client on understanding the opportunities for a new home entertainment technology, targeting everyday consumers. We were in the family's home to speak with them about their current gear and how they were using it.

In this house, the father had put a lot of effort into making product choices that would enhance their family's time together. He was visibly (and appropriately) proud of their setup. As he explained the choices he had made, he explained how he didn't want a DVR, or digital video recorder, because of his concerns over privacy. He referred to what was then well known as the leading DVR brand, TiVo, but mispronounced it as "Tye-vo."

"I took a look at Tye-vo but didn't want anyone paying attention to what we watch the way Tye-vo does so I decided that Tye-vo wasn't for us." As with many stories, this one has become richer in the retelling, but you can imagine how my client, originally an engineer, quietly winced each time the brand name was misspoken. I could sense his winces without turning my head to look at him. You can imagine when he heard "Tye vo" he saved that bit of information, but he didn't include the meta-information, like how this person pronounced that word.

The interview continued and when it was appropriate for me to ask follow-up questions about DVRs, I referred to it as the participant did—as Tye-vo. But later, when the client asked some of his own questions, he pronounced TiVo correctly as "tee-vo." My client was not intentionally correcting him, he just hadn't held onto the meta-information about the pronunciation. Still, this was a small, yet dramatic moment in the interview. This proud man was revealed to be, well, stupid, in front of his family, in his home. Despite being a self-proclaimed expert in these types of products, he was indirectly corrected and thus lowered in status. You could immediately feel the power dynamic in the room shift; now we were the experts, and he was just some dude. Of course, that's not the situation I was hoping for! It was better for me not to dwell on that moment and instead move on, but I might have tried defusing the awkwardness by reassuring everyone "I've heard it pronounced both ways."

My client was a wonderful, sweet, caring person who would never dream of making this participant feel that badly. But it would have never occurred to him to say something the "wrong" way. Yet in this situation, it was right to be wrong. It wasn't our role to be right.

Design researcher Todd Hausman talks about his work on an instant messaging product, when research participants would refer to "emo-chicons." In reflecting back their pronunciation, he was viscerally reminded of the risk in making assumptions about users.

Letting go of being right is something to pay attention to in most interviews; it doesn't have to be as glaring a situation as a participant's mispronunciation of a technology or a brand name. It could be in the description of a part, a process, or just about anything. Even if there's not an obvious "right" or "wrong" way to refer to something, you must defer to the participant's way.

> **NOTE** WHEN IT'S AWKWARD TO USE THEIR LANGUAGE
>
> It can be challenging to use someone else's terminology and feel as if you are being authentic. (After all, you are trying to establish rapport, and being fake would destroy that.) Participants in a study told us about a new technology that was being developed at their organization, called an *aggregator*. Due to its troubled history, it was referred to colloquially as an "aggravator." This term was used more frequently in the interview than "aggregator." But it wasn't comfortable for our interviewer to ask about the "aggravator." They didn't really have permission from the group to use their insider language, and they ran the risk of coming off as flippant or minimizing the seriousness of the development effort.

They resolved it by acknowledging the participant's language and their own reluctance to use the same phrase. Going a little meta (such as "I want to ask about what you like to call the aggravator") enables the interviewer to point to the language directly, acknowledging the participant's terminology, as well as referring back to the previous conversation about the terminology itself. When the words being used become a topic in the interview, pointing to the words in this manner is appropriate and can provide the authenticity the researcher needs.

In one project, a research participant referred to a technology platform their firm uses. Our client, perhaps trying to demonstrate insider status and reassure the participant that this interview was valid, asked about the platform but used an abbreviated form (a widely used nickname, like Mickey D's for McDonald's or AmEx for American Express) of the platform name. The participant responded by hesitantly using this nickname and then immediately correcting himself and switching back to the full name that he had originally used. If my client simply *had* to introduce his alternative name for the technology, he could have asked "Oh, when you say [platform name], I wonder if that's the same thing I'm used to calling [nickname]?" In this case, there would be no ambiguity, and he would not in any way be trying to clarify, so the better course of action would have been to build rapport by accepting the terms the participant was using rather than trying to demonstrate credibility.

Don't Make Your Questions Pass/Fail

A client joined me in the field, arriving at our pre-meeting with mere moments to get acquainted and review the approach. This was not an ideal arrangement (and a good learning moment for me) and led to a dysfunctional dynamic. Her abrupt questions for our participant were presented more as tests than as inquiries. She asked our participant if she knew what a USB cable was (see Figure 6.3), phrasing it as a challenge rather than as something she was curious about. Later, she presented her framework for the digital media functionality she was charged with designing and asked the participants if they understood the difference between the various terms used in the framework. The participant became confused and very uncertain about how to talk about her usage since these terms were indeed unfamiliar. It's good to understand if the language you are using internally aligns with the way people are really talking, but that doesn't mean you need to thrust your terms at people and test them on whether or not they can explain them.

Similarly, don't concoct convoluted scenarios and ask if people ever do them (or even worse, would want to do them). "Do you ever have a team meeting where some of the participants haven't completed their assigned pre-read, but you have to make a critical decision that stakeholders are expecting alignment on within a certain time frame?" These scenarios are hard to parse, and difficult to respond to, because you are asking about the specific combination of multiple factors that may not exist in that specific combination. When I see people ask those questions, it's usually not part of their effort to understand their participant's context on its own terms, but rather to try to see how suitable a preconceived solution might be for this participant.

People new to research sometimes declare their goal is to avoid leading questions, and yes, that's a worthy concern, but here the problem is less about how the questions are asked than the motivation for asking them to begin with.

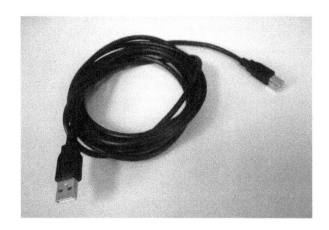

FIGURE 6.3
Do *you* know what a
USB cable is?

Don't Presume They Accept Your Worldview

I interviewed a young man who had gone through a significant personal change, first living abroad as a successful professional, and then returning to California to live in his parents' home to go back to school. At one point in the interview, my client commented to our participant (let's call him Keith) about the differences in value systems between "Old Keith" and "New Keith." Even though this is not a framework that Keith had explicitly articulated to us, he said, "Right."

After a few minutes of further dialogue, I decided it was time to intercede, and I asked Keith what he thought about this idea of the old versus new Keith. When finally given the chance to weigh in, Keith told us, "I don't really see it."

At no point had Keith told us that he had old and new versions of himself. Keith was always Keith. My client was synthesizing on-the-fly and had imposed his model on Keith. And what did Keith do? He agreed. Of course, he agreed! Why should he argue about something like that? Just because a framework isn't rejected by the participant doesn't mean it is accurate!

Don't Lecture

An alternative title here might be "Sit on your hands!" or "You don't need to give voice to every thought that comes into your head!" On a project that dealt with online decision support tools, one client, when offered the chance partway through the interview to follow up on the conversation so far, came up with this gem, presented here in sanitized form.

> I suppose that seems more like a divergent set of factors informing you versus specific feedback that came from any particular individual source and that served as a guiding factor for decisions for your purchase or not. I'm just thinking that it's more of a multiple…

At this point, the participant interrupted the client to tell us more about her decision-making process. Although sharing your forming thoughts *can* be a method of interrogation, it is a tricky approach, relying heavily on rapport and shared agenda to be effective. That was not what was happening here. The client didn't really say anything about anything but was just thinking aloud. Although I'm a huge enthusiast for sensemaking, it would have been fine for the client to have kept this in their head and declined to ask any questions.

But, within a minute of the exchange, the emboldened client continued, making declarative summary statements about the utility of a specific type of online tool. Their descent into lecture mode was complete; they were not asking questions and instead were sharing their own beliefs, in as confident a manner as possible. They had transformed from a listener to a teller.

If You Have to Fix Something, Wait Until the End

If you are interviewing someone about your product, it will be tempting to help them have the best experience possible. You will invariably watch them struggle to find features, express a desire for something that you know is available, or hear them describe aspects of the product incorrectly. This can be very trying for an interviewer who is also passionate about the product. (Of course, you are! After all, you are out in the field meeting customers in order to make the product better!) So how do you deal with this?

Do *not* jump in and correct or instruct them. This is just like the TiVo example, only more so! You are conducting the interview to learn from this person, so there's no need to assert your own expertise. In fact, once you do so, you can lose control over the interview entirely, as the participant will simply turn it around and ask you, "Is there a way to do_____? How can I make _____ happen?" Suddenly, your field visit has turned into the world's most expensive tech support house call.

By all means, at the end of the interview, as you are handing over the incentive and packing up, take a moment to share anything that you think might help that person. But ask yourself if explaining something is better for you or better for them. Don't correct their perceptions or terminology if the only outcome is "educating" them. Advocate for them, not for your product.

I led an interview with a fascinating professional who blew our minds with his insights into building up a professional network over decades of his career. As he was showing us how he worked, we saw him complain as he struggled to move the cursor between his two monitors, as the one on the left was set in Windows to be on the right. After we were finished, I offered to fix this, since it was something that came up peripherally in discussion. He was absolutely thrilled and quipped that this bit of support (even more than the incentive, or the tips my clients had given him about how to use their product) made the whole time worthwhile! Hyperbole or not, I was glad to be able to do something nice for him after he had been so wonderful to us.

In an episode of Marc Maron's *WTF* podcast, he spoke with 85-year-old comedy legend Jonathan Winters.[13] Within this interview are several examples that embody the points I've made throughout this chapter—getting to more of the answer, asking clarification questions, managing the ebb and flow of the interview, and not presuming that the participant accepts the interviewer's worldview.

Early in the interview, Maron asked a fairly direct question:

"You were in the Marines. Where were you?"

Winters answered:

"I went in at 17. The Japanese were way down on the list...Pearl Harbor. I didn't get along with either parent; they were divorced; it didn't seem to matter; they didn't like me."

His truth-in-comedy comment about his parents seemed to be a non-sequitur, and he continued on about his parents and some of his time in the Marines for more than three minutes (finally explaining that he was on an aircraft carrier, which answered Maron's question), before concluding with:

"But I enjoyed the Marines...I only made corporal, but that's okay..."

Maron picked up on the earlier non-sequitur and asked:

"Was it a way to get out of your parents' house?"

And Winters quipped back:

"Yeah, yeah, they were eager to sign. I never saw two people sign papers so fast!"

Although the answer to Maron's question was buried within several layers of stories, Winters only *implied* his motivation for enlisting. Maron did the right thing and asked his subject explicitly about it. As the interviewer, you want to find out for sure, from the subject's perspective, rather than leaving things to your own inferences.

continues

---

13 Marc Maron, "Episode 173, Jonathan Winters," *WTF* (podcast), May 9, 2011, www.wtfpod.com/podcast/episodes/episode_173_-_jonathan_winters (paywalled)

Later in the interview, Maron was less successful as an interviewer. Winters described an early job working as a radio DJ. In this job, he eventually got bored and did interviews with himself, playing different characters. Management objected, Winters persisted, and he was fired:

Winters: "I did try some more guests and that was the end of that career there."

Maron (laughing, interjected): "You had to, though, right?"

Winters: "I had to."

Maron: "Yeah! It felt too good, right?"

Winters: "It felt good. I did a year there, and then I went to Columbus."

Maron's interjections reflected his own interpretation: that Winters must have been compelled to continue doing interviews with himself because of how good it felt. Winters never actually said that, but Maron stated it as a fact, where his "right?" was not truly a question but more like a fellow bar patron elbowing you in the ribs while asking you to agree with him. What this transcription fails to capture is the momentum Winters had in telling his story, and even though he agreed with Maron, he was sidetracked from his story and ended up expressing parts of it in Maron's terms, not his own.

The Last Word

When you're out in the field, actually doing your interview, you will be relying on all of your question-asking skills. Your dexterity in choosing from and applying those skills will make a significant difference in the information you uncover.

- Your interview guide is a *guide*. Set it aside until you really need it. Leading the interview successfully comes down to *you*.

- Although it's tricky, ask the shortest question you can, without directing your participants to possible answers you are looking for. Then be silent.

- When you move from one topic to another, use transitional phrases such as "Great, I'd like to shift directions now....." or "Let's go back to something you said before....."

- Pay attention to whether or not you have received an answer to your question. Be prepared to follow up multiple times using different types of questions.

- Reflect back the language and terminology that your participant used (even if you think it was "wrong").

- If you want to fix something (say, a setting on their software) for your participant, wait until the interview is over.

Better Interviews

An interview is an interaction between two humans. Or maybe you can include your colleague and your participant's spouse, and now it's an interaction between four humans—irrational, emotional, language-using, unpredictable humans. The only one of these four you have any control over is yourself. There will always be variables and curve balls. This is a messy business.

Let's sit with that messiness for a moment. An interview comprises an enormous set of choices. No two researchers will make the same choices. We have our own brains, hearts, and histories.

And again, we're doing this work with other people, and it's impossible to predict how those people will connect, or not. Then you can factor in all the social and cultural dynamics that come into play. Factors like age, disability status, social status, gender presentation, race, ethnicity, and so on will create real complexity. The answer to any question is dependent not just on how the question is asked, but who is asking it, and who they are asking.

This chapter looks at some of the more common challenges that you will face in the field. It also suggests a number of ways to develop your own skills so that you are prepared for future surprises.

Troubleshooting Common Interview Problems

Many of the situations discussed in this section stem from something that happened leading up to the interview, such as how the participants were recruited. The best troubleshooting approach is to prevent these problems from occurring through proper screening and clear setting of expectations. Realistically, though, they will still come up.

When the Participant Is Reticent

Are you sure that your participant is holding back? As discussed in Chapter 6, "The Intricacies of Asking Questions," their default demeanor and speaking rhythm may simply be out of sync with yours.

If you conclude that they are indeed uncomfortable, try to identify the cause and make a change in the way you are handling the interview. You might simply need to accept the awkwardness and be patient with yourself and with them, looking toward a point where they become more comfortable. If they are connecting better with one of your colleagues, ask that person to lead the rest of the interview.

If there are too many interviewers, ask one of them to step back. If you aren't giving your participant enough verbal space to reflect and respond, slow down and let them talk. If your participant needs more structure, fall back to straightforward, direct questions.

Consider which aspects of your topic might be making your participant uncomfortable. Even if an interview doesn't explore obvious social taboos, you may be tapping into an element of personal insecurity about their job, competence, intelligence, and so on. Set your current topic aside for now and look for an opportunity to come back to it later.

Sometimes you might find yourself in a different situation than you had anticipated. For example, say an interview with a certain type of professional turns out to be an interview with that person *and* their manager. If you can't get the interview you want (perhaps by gently suggesting you interview each of them separately), be aware of the dynamics and adjust your questions appropriately. Ask the manager questions about themself or about their understanding of how the work is performed.

If all else fails, consider asking your participant outright to identify the source of their discomfort. Tell the participant that this information is important to you and your work and that you are deeply interested, but you are concerned that they aren't comfortable with the conversation. Ask what would be better, even if it means a different time or a different location.

When the Participant Isn't the Right Kind of User

Assuming you've screened your subject, you might wonder how that person can end up being wrong for the study. If you are surprised—or even uncomfortable—at how reality differs from what you expected, that's a crucial insight. But don't be hasty to dismiss the participant.

If you've taken the time to travel to this participant's home or workplace, you should complete the interview. Consider what you might do with the 45 minutes you could save by cutting out early and how that stacks up against the possibility that you might learn something by interviewing this person about their experience and perspective. Reset your expectations and see what you can get out of the session.

Afterward, revisit your screening criteria. You may have uncovered the fact that a word or phrase in the criteria is being interpreted differently by participants (for example, "late-model car" could mean one thing to your team and another to the people you are recruiting). Also, if you have identified additional factors for the rest of the participants, you might want to rescreen them.

NOTE **GETTING THE RIGHT PARTICIPANT AND THE RIGHT CONTEXT**

In several studies, I recruited participants who were users of various consumer electronics. They had told us they owned these devices and used them for whatever tasks we were interested in. But several times I found myself at the interview, discovering that the device in question wasn't actually at their home, where the interview was conducted. One person worked for an airline and had homes in two cities. Another person met us at his girlfriend's house, where none of his stuff was located. Another lived with roommates and her young children, while her computer was at the home of their father. And so on. After this happened a few times, I updated the language of my screener to ensure that the interview would take place in their primary residence and where the device was, and that they would be prepared to show us the device during the interview.

During another project, we were seeking people who were actively sharing certain types of information. One participant was indeed actively sharing this information, but only with his immediate family, with whom he lived some of the time. We hadn't specified that "sharing" should take place with a broader network, and even though we had reviewed the screener with our client, no one had seen this as a concern. From this interview, it emerged that we all had different ideas of what "sharing" meant. Our client was very concerned since they had conceived of sharing as a different behavior. In the interview itself, we focused on learning everything we could from this participant, but in the aftermath, we had a number of intense conversations with the client to determine whether or not this participant was acceptable for the study.

When the Participant Won't Stop Talking

As you settle into a rhythm with participants, you may realize that they talk extensively, requiring little or no prompting from you. Before you try to "fix" this issue, ask yourself whether this really is a problem. You have prepared extensively and have a lot of questions you're hoping to ask, but are you getting what you need from this participant? If you don't feel in control, you might be annoyed, but keep the emotional factor separate and assess the interview in terms of the information you need. In some cases, they won't be answering your questions at all. Give them space to tell the story they've chosen to tell you and then redirect them back to your question. For example, consider the following exchange, which is drawn from a real experience:

Q: "What kind of food do you prepare for yourself?"

A: "When I was a child [long story about her mother, etc., etc.]"

Q: "So how does that experience as a child impact the decisions you make now for your family?"

Your last resort is to interrupt. If you must interrupt, frame it appropriately—"Excuse me! I'm so sorry to interrupt, but I know we have a limited amount of time, and I want to make sure we cover the topics we're here to learn about."

When you find yourself in this situation, you have to adjust how you are going to use your guide. If you ordinarily would use three or four questions (along with brief follow-ups, clarifications, and so on) to set context and dig into your key topic, you should instead be more directive and less open-ended. If each question generates five minutes of nonstop response, it won't work to ask questions that are intended to produce short answers. You have to shift to the (normally less-desirable) closed-ended question.

While most interviews might go like this:

Setting context question: "What's led to your current design for your workspace?"

A: "I realized I had to get serious about the space, so I got this lamp and this microphone. Umm, the couch, but we took that out, there's this shelf, and I've got a new chair here."

Specific topic of interest question: "Do you think any of these have affected your productivity at work?"

A: "Oh definitely, I'd say the chair, oh and probably the microphone, because . . . "

Occasionally, you end up with this dynamic, where your context-setting question runs away.

Setting context question: "What's led to your current design for your workspace?"

A: "When we moved in here, we rehabbed all the rooms, and this room was the last one on the list, but I made it a priority to select new accessories and furniture. We had a couch in here, but my daughter was spending more time practicing her piccolo, so we needed to give her ergonomic support so we moved that couch out, and I thought maybe a sofa bed would go here, but we don't like futons—after college life, we said no futons ever again...they really aren't good for sleeping or sitting and so I don't know...why do people buy them?"

If that happens, ask more directive questions, jumping directly to the specific topic of interest:

Q: "Can you tell me the top two or three items in this room that have had a positive effect on your work productivity?"

A: "The chair is crucial to me because it's where I spend most of my time, on calls, or reading. I use this microphone for those calls and now that people can hear me well, I feel like I'm making more effective personal connections, you know?"

FROM MY PERSPECTIVE

CONFERENCE INTERRUPTUS

I was at a conference in Bangalore. The last session of the day included a fairly spirited Q&A. There were two microphones going around the audience, and while another audience member and a panelist were going back and forth on one mic, I got the other. The discussion was falling apart; the audience member was fixated on some issue and was not going to let it go, but there was no resolution. The conversation had devolved into posturing and deflection. People began to get annoyed and mutter and shift in their seats. They saw me with the microphone and began, quietly at first and then more insistently, to encourage me to interrupt.

I could see that interrupting was within the norm for this culture, but even as I was standing up and being cheered on, it was extremely difficult for me to interrupt. I succeeded in opening my mouth, but nothing came out. Twice. Meanwhile, the droning, time-wasting, back-and-forth continued, and my fellow attendees were losing patience with me. Finally, I was able to interrupt, but it was a significant challenge, even with all the affirmation! In an interview, I find interrupting almost as difficult and do it only when I absolutely have to. ■

When the Participant Won't Stick to the Topic

When someone diverges from what you think the topic is, let relevance be your guide. The guidance is similar to the previous example where a question about food leads to a story about their mother: consider whether the answer provides more context to the original topic, and if needed, ask them to make the connection back to the issue at hand.

Without cues from you, people may not know what it is that you want to talk about. They've built a certain idea based on the process through which they were invited to participate and what you said when you began the interview. If you represent an organization that they have a relationship with, that's going to inform what they expect to talk about.

Here, you can use some of the tools in rapport building to guide and redirect the interview. If your participant brings up MangoTech (your company) while you are trying to understand what their job responsibilities entail, don't follow up on that! At this point in the interview, don't follow their cues, but instead demonstrate what you are interested in by asking more questions about what you want to cover. The less you acknowledge verbally or otherwise, the stronger your message will be.

If you find that isn't sufficient, you should next try acknowledging and redirecting, "I gather you've had some experience with Mango-Tech, and we're going to get to that in a bit, but I'd love to get some context first." (Or "Let's see if we have time at the end to hear about that as well but for the most part, I'd love to focus on....") When they do focus on your desired topics, you might gently amplify how you convey interest and enthusiasm to further contrast your total lack of response to the topics you are not interested in.

When You Feel the Participant Isn't Being Truthful

It's important to distinguish between two different situations: people who deliberately mispresent themselves in order to be part of your study in order to get that easy user research incentive money versus people who are inconsistent or trying to manage how they are perceived.

The first is deliberate and malicious. Your recruiting and screening process should try to filter those people out, but you're still going to have this happen. It's only happened to me a few times, but I often wonder at the moment whether it's a misunderstanding between the participant and the recruiter or between the recruiter and me. Outright deception seems so incongruous, especially as this person is sitting and answering my questions and acting as if they truly are the person they are presenting themselves as. For example, I interviewed a very forthcoming Silicon Valley executive in his home, as he described his side business in a way that utterly, distressingly contradicted what he had told the recruiter. If you have some way to be certain that something is awry, then wrap up early, but I tend to stick it out because in the interview itself, I'm just not sure.

The second is natural. People may tell you they value cleanliness and then open a bedroom door to reveal piles of dirty clothes on the floor. Or people may express a preference for a certain type of feature and then reject an example you show them. Although you might find this frustrating, try to see it as an opportunity. Your interpretation of "cleanliness" may be oversimplified. The social performance of valuing cleanliness may be entirely separate from the act of maintaining cleanliness. Your framework for what that feature is doing may not align with the participant's framework. These seeming disconnects are indications that you need to explore further. This isn't about calling out "hypocrisy"; it's about probing to understand.

I've seen far too many articles and conference talks that refer to this very human dynamic as "lying." This edgy-seeming framing lacks compassion and doesn't serve your research objective at all. Instead, start with the assumption (as an early mentor would remind me) that *your participant makes sense*, and go from there.

When You Feel Uncomfortable or Unsafe

Unless you are going to a public or familiar corporate location, don't conduct interviews on your own. When you arrive at a location, verify that everyone feels safe. Pay attention to the difference between *unsafe* and *uncomfortable*.[1] If you feel unsafe, don't go in. If you feel uncomfortable, try to set that feeling aside and proceed (see Figures 7.1 and 7.2). Of course, how any of us make that assessment

---

1   See Steve Portigal, "Let's Embrace Open-Mindedness," *Johnny Holland*, June 19, 2009, https://web.archive.org/web/20120610222212/https://johnnyholland .org/2009/06/lets-embrace-open-mindedness/. (Scroll to "Getting Out of the Comfort Zone") for some thoughts about acknowledging people's discomfort in new or different situations. Coming to grips with this discomfort is a wonderful way to grow as an interviewer.)

is based on our own experiences, biases, privilege, status, and so on, and in a team situation, it's highly possible that different backgrounds will lead to a different perspective on safety versus discomfort. You should be prepared to accommodate the concerns of your teammates, especially when they differ from yours.

FIGURE 7.1
Check your gut reaction. If you feel uncomfortable, it may still be okay to proceed.

FIGURE 7.2
If you feel unsafe, pay attention to that feeling and stay away from dangerous places.

There will be plenty of strange interviews. It's an hour or two of your life; if you aren't in danger, do your best to learn what you need to learn, acknowledge that life is interesting, and add the experience to your set of stories.[2]

If you feel increasing discomfort in response to someone else's behavior, take a moment to pause and identify what's happening. You might want to call for a bathroom break. If you are at risk, leave. Otherwise, you can ignore the behavior (but not the person) or restate your objectives and give the participant the opportunity to agree to continue with that focus. Of course, be aware of your own limits and be prepared to leave if the situation deteriorates.

Patriarchy, white supremacy, and racism are deeply rooted and generally unavoidable aspects of culture. Women and people of color can feel unsafe when they encounter sexist and racist treatment in many parts of their lives, including fieldwork. In *Doorbells, Danger, and Dead Batteries*,[3] Raffaella Roviglioni shared a story about how her participant assumed that her male assistant was actually the one in charge, and Lindsay Moore described how when she and two female colleagues visited a participant in his home, he immediately expressed interest in seeing them unclothed. Alba Villamil and Crystal Yan organized a panel discussion about "Race in the Field"[4] that highlighted some of their experiences and the challenges in addressing them (e.g., white colleagues stepping in can actually lower the perceived status of someone who is a target of racist behavior).

---

2 Danger can be a personally subjective issue. In this video, https://vimeo.com/9217883, Luis Arnal describes his design-research adventures, including arranging with gang leaders to gain access to Brazilian slums (known as *favelas*) for fieldwork, the consequences of inadvertently photographing an FBI undercover operation, and (if not dangerous then perhaps uncomfortable) participating in one of Spencer Tunick's massive nude photo shoots.

3 Steve Portigal, *Doorbells, Danger, and Dead Batteries: User Research War Stories* (New York: Rosenfeld Media, 2016), 123, (especially Chapter 8, "The Perils of Fieldwork").

4 See a summary at Crystal Yan, "Navigating User Research as Designers of Color," *Discovery* (newsletter), February 10, 2021.

By Joyce Kakariyil Paul, Ph.D.

Joyce is a human experience authority who thrives on executing creative ways to bridge the human vs. technology gap. She is also a performing artist (arpanarts.org) and painter who founded her non-profit SCARF (scarf.global) that aims to create and foster art that brings awareness around social issues to galvanize change.

Our jobs as user researchers, by definition, might be about understanding the needs, preferences, and behaviors of the people who use or might use a product or service, but to me it is a powerful way of learning about different mindsets, cultures, backgrounds, and perspectives that define how and why people interact with technology. It becomes even more amazing when we step away from the comfort of remote surveys and usability labs to conduct ethnographic research.

But it's not easy. It can take a lot physically and emotionally, especially when compared to sitting in an air-conditioned corporate lab, with clear access to free drinks and snacks! We are now stepping into people's lives—observing them in their natural settings and often shadowing them in their daily jobs, activities, and routines.

Imagine following a UPS driver as they drive door-to-door with a small scanner app that shows nothing at all in the bright sunlight or an Amazon delivery person expecting to see "drop-off details" on their app while walking all around a house, trying not to look like a stalker, or a doctor as they conduct surgeries with Da Vinci robot arms. It is super cool *and* super hard.

It is super hard because I encounter the challenges and biases that affect my work and my well-being. We continue to be challenged by a lack of diversity and representation in the user research field and in the tech industry in general. As an older, female, person of color with an Indo-British accent, I often feel like I am the only one who looks and sounds like me in the room. Stereotypes and assumptions about my identity, my skills, and my role follow me every single day. Usually, these cognitive and cultural biases crop up when I meet someone for the very first time. I believe this is primarily because we are hard-wired by evolution to assess an unfamiliar entity in our environment, in order to ensure our survival in the wild. We humans can't escape or voluntarily stop the judgment track started by our hind brains.

continues

Let me share a story: I am a performing artist during weekends and the organizers of a local performing arts festival were coming to pick me up. I had told them to pick me up outside building 30 at Microsoft. Their van drew up. They saw me waiting, leaning against my parked Honda, but completely bypassed me! Here is an Indian-looking woman, standing next to a stereotypical immigrant car outside a Microsoft building, so she has to be a tech worker, right? Can't be the artist we are supposed to pick up, right?

Another example took place earlier in my career. I spent six months going through many rounds of permission letters and approvals in order to conduct fieldwork in a very prestigious human performance lab. As soon as I completed my pilot study, I was approached inappropriately by the lab's director. I was given the choice to either comply or to leave the lab. I complained to my supervisor and the general manager of this reputable laboratory, but ultimately, I had to change my project and embark on something different. I'm not sure if the director that harassed me faced any consequences beyond a rap on his knuckles, but I have never regretted that decision, both as a human being and as a researcher/anthropologist!

One of the challenges of doing ethnographic research is ensuring safety and comfort for both the researcher and the participants. In my educational and professional experiences, I have travelled alone to remote locations, stayed awake on overnight train journeys because I was afraid to sleep, had my bags and equipment stolen during one study, had a host make sexual advances at me, and survived drinking water out of a well where frogs swam!

We often fail to ask these questions as part of project scoping or the research plan:

1. Does the gender (among other characteristics such as race, language, age, clothing, etc.) of the researcher affect the success of execution?

2. Can the researcher access certain physical locations or demographies?

3. Can access to field sites be negotiated and/or can a connecting link help with establishing rapport with prospective participants?

4. Are there cultural or social barriers in conducting research (whether it's a shorter interview or an all-day shadowing activity)?

5. Does informed consent, confidentiality, reciprocity, and power dynamics work the same way in different geographies and when studied by researchers of different ethnicities?

All of these affect the safety and well-being of the researcher and could unknowingly affect the quality and validity of the research data.

As a researcher, I take on many different roles, and each of them has different implications for how I think about safety. I may even choose a different approach to the study because of these safety considerations.

- Am I the observer or the participant?
- Am I the insider in a tribe or the outsider who is conducting the research?
- Am I the formal/official researcher with a clipboard, pencil, and camera or a friend that worked on building a relationship enough to become a participant observer?
- Am I the impartial analyzer/**data interpreter** or the biased **human** peeking her head behind the garb of an impartial researcher?

The more open I have been to experiences and possibilities, the more precious my insights have been. I have learnt to adapt to any personal discomfort that is part of the practice and ethos of my participant. It is their world, and they have been kind enough to have me peek at it. I am honored.

THE MINOR MELTDOWN

After a few long days of fieldwork, my client and I headed to Los Angeles's Toy District to interview a wholesaler. Driving separately (as he was heading to the airport afterward), we had each struggled naïvely through traffic the way that out-of-towners do when searching for parking. I left my car in a no-parking spot and went to verify our meeting location. Our interview was with a small business owner. I was picturing a typical retail setting, with a familiar storefront, street numbers, etc. Instead, I found a street filled with stalls, jammed with merchandise, on a street with few prominent building numbers (many were just scrawled in marker on the outer edges of the stalls). Something about this did not feel right, so I called our recruiter and got confirmation that we were indeed in the right place.

I left my car in a lot and walked to meet my client, who was still in his car, circling. I got into his car and relayed my impressions as he navigated traffic, still looking for parking. The long days, the daunting traffic, the unfamiliar surroundings, and the parking problems had been accumulating until something within him snapped. He turned red, made a sudden turn, and floored his accelerator. Fortunately for me, his venting of emotions gave me space to be "the calm one" (although no doubt I had fed his anxiety with my own). We drove a few blocks, and I made some very concrete suggestions about where to park. Once calmness returned, we both could see that there was nothing really wrong, but we had just reached the end of our ropes. We got some food and walked back to our interview. We were overwhelmed and exhausted, and the lack of familiarity caused a brief and intense descent into fear. That experience with the fight-or-flight reflex helped me more finely parse the difference between discomfort and danger. ◼

Interview Variations and Special Cases

While I've devoted much of this book to the optimal case, where you and your participant have arranged the best possible interview situation, there are inevitably exceptions. In this section, I'll show you how to deal with some of these situations:

- When your interview is in a market research facility
- When your interview is very short
- When your participant can't be interrupted
- When your organization has a relationship with the participant
- Interviewing professionals vs. consumers
- Interviewing multiple participants

When Your Interview Is in a Market Research Facility

Focus group companies offer meeting rooms designed for market research, with mirrored-wall observation rooms, video recording, and all the other accoutrements. It would be a mistake to consider these facilities as neutral third places. When you invite people to come to a facility to be interviewed, they are coming to *your* house. Unfortunately, all the comfy couches, Nerf balls, and tasty snacks don't change that. You must be the host instead of the guest. Even if you don't feel settled in this new environment yourself, you must welcome them into your space. You can ask them to bring something of their own (photos, artifacts, or a collage) to the interview, but this approach is a definite compromise.

Some companies have built their own research spaces, perhaps with special arrangements with building security so it's easier for people to get in. This location is still entirely *your* environment, familiar to you but not your participant. No matter how welcoming you are, there's a tremendous power imbalance for consumers coming into your branded, designed space. Again, you must be the host.

Remote research, when the researcher is working from home, "gives the participant as much a window into my world as it does theirs" notes researcher Shannon Stoll. This has the potential to make the shared remote context more equal: you are in each other's houses.

When Your Interview Is Very Short

If you can only schedule a short amount of time with people, warm them up before the interview. Get them thinking about your topics by emailing them some key questions to think about. They don't need to write up their answers ahead of time; they can just be reflecting on these topics and be prepared to share some perspective. You won't have time to probe too much, so your interview needs to really cut to the chase: ask them about the thing they are doing, how they are doing it, when they are doing it, and maybe even why they are doing it. Stick to your agreed-upon time unless they offer to talk longer, and then make an explicit request for a follow-up interview.

When Your Participant Can't Be Interrupted

If your participant is fully focused on their activity (such as working on an assembly line or a trading floor), possible adaptations to your approach might be the following:

- Use shadowing and observation (from Chapter 3, "Contextual Methods: More Than Just Asking Questions").
- Arrange for a brief or debrief-style interview before or after, or even on a separate visit.
- In a follow-up visit, review video of their initial activity and ask them to reflect and narrate what was happening at that time.
- Ask if they are able to narrate what they are doing as it happens.
- Sit with a subject-matter expert who can narrate what they are observing.
- If they can be briefly interrupted (say, between discrete tasks), your questions might primarily be "What just happened?" and "What's going to happen next?"
- Conduct multiple sessions over a period of time with the same participant.

When Your Organization Has a Relationship with the Participant

If you are interviewing enterprise customers, there's a business relationship at stake. There will be multiple perspectives around that relationship and how the interview itself should go: the participant who is a customer, the in-house researcher, the consultant researcher, the salesperson or other relationship owner, and so on. The customer may have shared information about your topic before, or about other concerns or requests. They may have open support issues. They may have participated in research about this or another topic before. The more you understand that previous history, the less likely you are to upset them (for example, "I've told you guys this 25 times already!"). You'll need to establish context for this conversation (both when you ask for the time and when you begin the session), and to make clear how you will follow up to help them get their concerns resolved, wherever possible. That existing relationship challenges the idea of being neutral, so plan how you will compartmentalize your commitment to the relationship and to the research.

If you are interviewing employees on behalf of their employer, there can be different legal requirements around the intention of the research, the employee's expectations around participating, and data privacy. Work with human resources and legal to set up a process that is acceptable to them.

In the interviews themselves, if you are *not* an employee of the company, make that clear to the participant to limit the internal jargon and references (or at least to set the expectation that you'll be asking for clarification when those come up). If you *are* an employee of the company, try to cultivate an outsider's perspective so that you can unpack references. If your participant says "Ahh…that rollout was terrible last quarter," rather than assuming that you know what rollout they are referring to and that you also know why it was terrible for them, ask for clarification: "Why did *you* see it as terrible?"

The Differences in Interviewing Professionals vs. Consumers

Consumer interviews (or *B2C*, if you prefer) typically take place in their home. When interviewing professionals (or *B2B* interviews), you might find yourself on a trading floor, in a hospital, in a restaurant, in an office, in a manufacturing facility, or in any other kind of work environment. Interviewing people at work may involve a combination of observation, shadowing, and interviewing. Depending on what you need to do when interviewing professionals, you need to be very specific in your interview request—duration of the session, environment you want to be in, role of the person you want to meet, and so on.

Consumers might default to treating your interview like a *visit*. Professionals often frame the interview as a *meeting*. You can choose to operate within those expectations, or you can seek to shift them, but keep in mind where your participant is coming from—what they expect from you, and what they expect the session to be like.

Interviewing Multiple Participants

We often ask other family members to join interviews, or we may speak to colleagues simultaneously when interviewing professionals. This is best done when you aren't expecting power dynamics to significantly impact the interview (such as a subordinate being asked to explain his career goals in front of his boss, or a teen being asked about her alcohol consumption in front of her parents). If need be, you can break the interview into separate chunks for each participant individually and for the group together.

In terms of group dynamics, your goal should be to get the participants talking extemporaneously, even to each other. Do not conduct two parallel identical interrogations; instead, gently lead a conversation by throwing your questions open and using eye contact and specific probes directed at individuals to encourage them to contribute. As you hold back, they will step forward.

Instead of this:

Interviewer: "When did you start drinking Kombucha?"

P1: "About six months ago."

Interviewer: "How about you, when did you start drinking Kombucha?"

P2: "It was about four months ago."

Interviewer: "And what is it about Kombucha that draws you to it?"

P1: "I like the taste."

Interviewer: "What about you?"

P2: "I like the way I feel after."

Aim for this:

Interviewer: "When did you each start drinking Kombucha?"

P1: "About six months ago."

Interviewer: [Pause]

P2: "Oh, for me it was about four months ago."

Interviewer: "And what is it about Kombucha?"

P1: "I like the taste."

P2: "You do? I actually can't stand the taste but...I like the way I feel after."

P1: "But tell them about what happened when you drank that tiny bottle last week!"

You'll have more success with people who already know each other. As I mentioned earlier when considering the number of interviewers, people influence each other simply by being together.[5] The more people you include, the more you'll experience that effect.

Using Different Interviewing Techniques at Different Points

Regardless of your business objectives, you always want to understand how the participant makes sense of the world and what problems and concerns they have. You may be early in the development process and have broad questions, or you may be further along and have hypotheses (concepts, animations, storyboards, designs, wireframes, and more). In the latter case, spend the first part of the interview understanding the participant's workflow, objectives, pain points, and so on. Then, when you share the artifacts you've brought, you'll have a better chance of understanding *why* they are responding the way they do. If you aren't interested in that amount of detail and just want reactions to your prototype, you're better off doing usability testing, not interviews.

Improving as an Interviewer

Now that you've learned more techniques for interviewing, you can hone and refine your performance further by practicing, reflecting, critiquing, collecting, and sharing. Earlier, I mentioned the individualistic nature of research, that we all come to it with unique backgrounds and life experiences. Even though no two researchers will conduct an interview the same way, that isn't to say it's up to chance—it's not. No two actors will deliver one of Hamlet's soliloquies the same, but all their studying and rehearsing sets them up to do their particular best.

---

5   For more, see either "Asch Conformity Experiments," Wikipedia, Wikimedia Foundation, http://en.wikipedia.org/wiki/Asch_conformity_experiments or "Normative Social Influence," Wikipedia, Wikimedia Foundation, http://en.wikipedia.org/wiki/Normative_social_influence.

Practice

Yes, right now you're reading a whole book with top-quality guidance, but all this cutting-edge brilliance only really sticks when *you* practice it for yourself. Interviewing is like any skill: the more you practice, the better you get. Even the busiest researcher only gets to do a certain number of interviews, so be creative in generating or finding other opportunities to practice. Take advantage of brief everyday encounters (say, that loquacious taxi driver) and do a little bit of interviewing, asking questions and follow-up questions. Cultivate a style of interacting socially that emphasizes listening, reflecting back the other person's comments, allowing for silence, and so on. Try for longer and deeper conversations to build up your stamina.

When you are in the field, remember that each interview is also a learning experience. Try something different once in a while. For example, use the interview guide from back to front while still maintaining rapport and keeping a comfortable flow; force yourself to count to five before everything you say; if you don't normally take notes, instead of just taking *some* notes, go all in and take *copious* notes.

Reflect

You can get the most out of any interview by reflecting on it. Football coaches review game films, and user researchers can take a similar approach. You have the material: audio, video, or transcripts. Otherwise, conduct and capture mock interviews specifically for this purpose. Look for moments that went well or moments that went slightly awry and think about what you would do differently. Don't beat yourself up about how you handled it in the moment; the benefit of reflection is that you can stop time and consider a range of options.

Seek out opportunities to be interviewed yourself. Although phone surveys or online customer satisfaction surveys use a different method, the participants aren't thinking about that; they are just being asked questions. Sign up for market research databases or volunteer for grad student studies. Go through the experience and notice when it feels bad (and anytime it feels right). You can use these insights to avoid, or replicate, such interview techniques.

Leverage your past experiences with strangers, such as going on blind dates, working as a bartender or waiter, being interviewed for a job, and more. What principles did you develop in those situations? Consider what worked and what didn't and why.

Critique

In addition to reviewing your own interviews, review other people's, too (and ask them to review yours). Tag along during a colleague's or mentor's interviews, pay attention to their technique, and ask them about it afterward. Teach someone else how to lead an interview. Or ask someone to come along to your interviews and get their feedback. Also ask for feedback from the rest of your field team (even if you are the lead interviewer), or even from your research participants.

Compare and Contrast

Check out interviews in the media: Terry Gross, Michael Barbaro, David Marchese, and Marc Maron are good places to start (see Figure 7.3). Watch and listen as an interviewer, not just an audience member. Although the context of journalism (writ large) differs from user research, you will notice techniques, both new and familiar. Even better, the podcast *The Turnaround*[6] is a set of interviews with journalists about their approach to interviewing.

FIGURE 7.3

Marc Maron is a comedian, not a journalist. His interviews (see Chapter 6) are a good source of both positive and negative examples.

---

6   Episodes available wherever you get your podcasts, or at https://maximumfun .org/podcasts/the-turnaround-with-jesse-thorn/

Learn from Mistakes

This book features plenty of examples of blunders and missteps by interviewers, including me. Seeing someone else's mistakes (as well as our own) is an effective way to learn about the sometimes-subtle tactics for interviewing users. Life provides us with an inexhaustible supply of those lessons! It's useful to observe others making mistakes (and also being successful), but I consistently make mistakes myself and usually try to learn from them. When you experience mishaps and screwups (of your own making or of someone else's), do your best to move past the frustration and self-recrimination into reflection, and then set a better intention for next time.

Tell Stories

For many years I've been gathering and publishing stories by other user researchers about their real-world fieldwork experiences.[7] These stories show how research can actually be an exciting activity that is interpersonal, intimate, and unpredictable, even though it is often hard work. Let's face it—even experienced people may find themselves in situations they aren't prepared to deal with. The more we share stories of failure, the more we normalize thoughtful and transparent consideration of our work.

These stories are tremendously valuable. By reading these stories, you can learn from what went wrong for someone else (or at least what was different than expected). By sharing these stories, you can create an opportunity for researchers to reflect more deeply on what really happens in the field. This is a way of addressing the personal qualities that researchers work on bolstering their entire lives. There are no tactical solutions for most of the challenges encountered in war stories. Sometimes a solution isn't necessary or even appropriate. Rather, there are things that can be learned only when things go awry.

Sharing these stories teaches you that research isn't a method executed on subjects; rather, it's an experience that people have together. Some of the priceless data that comes out of being in the field—the elements that aren't "findings"—are the ways in which you are personally and permanently changed. When you step outside of your comfort zone, you are heading off to war, in a small but meaningful way. You are facing two stages of risk—the first from whatever

---

7 I even wrote a whole book about this—from which this section is adapted: Portigal, *Doorbells, Danger, and Dead Batteries*.

unknown awaits you out there, and the second from the likelihood that you will return from the war forever changed.

Risk be damned, being changed is integral to the work we seek to do. Uncovering a new way of looking at the world, of understanding the beliefs and desires of a group of people represents a change in ourselves. Being changed, we advocate for that understanding, exhorting and cajoling others to grasp the nuances of that understanding, so that they can bring new things into the world that will better support others. In risking being changed, we are changed. And so, we try to change others, and we try to make something that changes the world for some.

And More...

Take an improv class. Improv training helps develop many aspects of interviewing, such as being in the moment, holding back judgment, and listening.[8] Meditation can help you be present during interviews and develop the mental energy it takes to focus deeply on someone else.

Connect with other interviewers online and at conferences. Read books about interviewing (Hey, you're doing that right now! Well done!) and about interpersonal communication.[9] As you learn more, you'll identify your own personal style and adjust for it.

---

8   I've given a number of talks about improv in the context of design and user research, such as Steve Portigal, "Yes, My Tuatara Loves to Cha-Cha: Improv, Creativity and Design," *UX New Zealand*, 2015, www.youtube.com/watch?v=Z-ByOul0rbc

9   For example, Deborah Tannen, *That's Not What I Meant* (New York: Harper, 2011).

The Last Word

Interviewing is made of people, and as such, your experiences in the field are going to be unpredictable and surprising. Be prepared for what might go awry and how you will deal with it.

- If you feel your participant is reticent, be sure it's not just a difference between their speaking rhythm and yours. Try to identify what's making them uncomfortable and make adjustments. If necessary, ask about any possible discomfort. Or just accept the awkwardness and move forward until they open up.

- You may not initially feel a participant is right for the study. Once you are there having the interview, stick with it. If the person isn't what you expected (despite deliberate screening), that is something worth reflecting on later; meanwhile, what can you learn from that person now?

- If you think your participant is talking too much, ask yourself if that's because you are feeling out of control or because you aren't getting the information you want. If you must interrupt, apologize and remind them that you value their limited time.

- In a phone interview, lack of visual cues makes it harder to adjust your pace and rhythm to the participant's. Give them an extra beat and give yourself permission to feel awkward in those small moments of silence or overlap.

- If you only have a very brief amount of time for your interview, prime your participant ahead of time with some questions or topics you plan to discuss.

- When interviewing several people at once, avoid asking each person the same question in turn and use eye contact to create a more free-flowing dialogue where some questions are addressed to an individual while others are thrown to the group. Allow them to follow up on each other's points and even ask each other questions.

- Be aware of the difference between discomfort and fearing for your safety. Develop a tolerance for the former, but do not compromise on the latter.

- Improve your interviewing skills by practicing, varying from your habitual approach, reviewing transcripts and videos, and seeking critiques from others.

CHAPTER 8

Documenting the Interview

On one level, documentation is how you capture the definitive, fully detailed record of the interview (the "data"). On another level, it's how you, as the interviewer, make the ah-has, and other important takeaways, stick. While doing this, you have to stay engaged with the participant. Beyond that, documentation also bleeds into the sensemaking and storytelling that follow fieldwork.

Taking Notes

Although you might be tempted to try, you simply can't catch everything by taking notes. Typical handwriting is about 30 words per minute, and a great typist can do 60 wpm. Audio books are at least 100 wpm (and likely closer to 150 wpm). But people speak less clearly—and more quickly—than in an audio book. The cold math tells us it's just not possible to get everything down. Add the high cognitive load of leading an interview, and you're done for. As transcriptionist Jo Ann Wall put it, "It can be a challenge to listen purposefully in order to determine matters of importance and screen out extraneous information."

You do need to get *everything*. In the moment, you will miss details, misconstrue intent, or mishear a word. It's important to have an accurate version of the interview to go back to. The bottom line is that you should be recording your interviews—something I talk more about in more detail in "Audio Recording the Interview," later in this chapter.

While I prefer to focus entirely on my interaction with the participant, some people find that taking notes helps them filter, synthesize, and ultimately better remember what is being discussed. The act of writing notes helps them process what is happening. They come away from the interview with pages and pages of handwritten rough notes. If you do this, remember that you must maintain eye contact while writing. Don't rely too heavily on asking your participants to wait while you catch up with what they've said. Worse still, you don't want to evoke the clichéd therapist who is bent into their notebook, muttering "mmm-hmm" and never looks up. By the same token, avoid overly signaling what you are interested in by scribbling furiously in response to certain types of input or response.

If, like me, you don't benefit from the act of note-taking, you can assign this task to another researcher who joins you (or even a third party who is simply tasked with documentation). As you include other forms of documentation, you can easily become overwhelmed with devices and tasks outside leading the interview itself, so consider what can be assigned to a supporting interviewer.

As mentioned in the previous chapter, you can also take notes about what you want to remember during the interview, as a way to manage the expanding tree of the interview, as well as jot down topics you want to come back to.

FROM MY PERSPECTIVE

(MIS)INTERPRETATIONS IN THE MOMENT

In one interview, I asked a participant, "If you and your wife own one iPod, how do you determine who is going to use it?" He responded, "Well, for commuting, it's either the iPod or the *New Yorker*." Two different scenarios are likely—1. She takes the iPod on the train, and he drives the car, a *New Yorker*, or 2. Whoever takes the iPod gets to listen to music, and the spouse gets to read the most recent issue of the *New Yorker* magazine. I didn't get to ask a clarification question, and it wasn't until I went back to the video that it was clear that he was referring to the magazine.

In that same session, the participant, talking about iPods and design told us, "Well, when you do that, it looks more Zen. It actually looks like the competition" and another participant added, "Yes, it's like he says, very Zen, very Japanese, very spiritual." The first participant was using the word "Zen" to refer to another brand of music players that was around at the time, called the Creative Zen. But the second participant (who may not have even been aware of that brand) heard that word and made their own connection to Zen Buddhism. Misinterpretations in the moment are inevitable, so you need proper documentation of what was said, so you can tease out what was meant. ■

NOTE-TAKING FOR PODCASTING

By Jorge Arango

Jorge Arango is an information architect, author, and educator. He is the host of The Informed Life *podcast.[1]*

Podcast interviews are like research interviews. Both require prompting another person for insightful information while remaining engaged and open. Note-taking also plays a key role in both.

I say "note-taking" as if it were a single thing, but I take different types of notes at different stages of the process. I use three different note-taking methods during podcasting that are also useful for research.

First, during interview sessions, I take notes using pen and paper. The point of these handwritten notes isn't capturing phrases verbatim. (I can't write fast enough to do that anyway.) Instead, their purpose is threefold:

1. Capturing phrases that remind me of important things the person has said.

2. Capturing follow-up questions that come to mind while the person is speaking.

3. Keeping my hands busy, which helps me focus on what the person is saying.

The challenge is to strike a good balance between paying attention to the notebook and the other person's voice. I aim to move fast on the page, capturing only short phrases or little sketches. I want to devote as much of my attention to the other person as possible. While I save these notes for the record, I don't have much use for them once the interview is over. For me, they are of most value during the session itself, so I can be more present as an interviewer.

Second, when I'm done with the interview, I import the audio files to an application called *Descript* that transcribes the conversation. Descript lets me edit the underlying audio tracks by changing the transcript text, which speeds up production.

After that, my assistant, Sarah, reviews and cleans up any errors in the transcript. She also adds logical breaking points between topics in the conversation, which she labels as section headings. When she's done, I do a final pass by reviewing and copyediting the transcripts and producing the final audio.

---

1   https://theinformed.life/

Later, I will write a blog post that summarizes the interview. So, while editing the transcript, I look to understand the conversation's structure. I also take notes about the main points and highlight paragraphs or phrases that illustrate key issues. Some of those notes get copied-and-pasted directly into the blog post. These highlights and notes serve as a distillation of the conversation. They remind me of what we discussed and what mattered, which is essential since we often edit shows many weeks after we recorded the interview. I've had mixed results so far with AI-generated summaries. It's a good starting point, but it's nothing I'd publish without significant rewriting. Still, AI holds a lot of promise here, so I keep experimenting.

The third approach to note-taking operates at a level above the other two. I've only done it once, but it was a powerful (if time-consuming) experience that I'll likely repeat at some other point. To produce a "year in review" episode, I planned to go through the 24 interviews from that year to find common themes. Then I'd weave snippets from relevant conversations into a single episode that highlighted those themes through many voices.

I started with the interview transcripts and moved them into a note-taking application. I broke up each section of each transcript into a separate note and then looked at those notes visually, as though I was working with sticky notes on a whiteboard. I discarded some notes and grouped others into clusters. The biggest clusters became the themes to highlight in the episode.

From here, I pulled together a script for the episode and then copied the relevant audio snippets into a new sequence. I also recorded brief interstitials between them that added context and gave the conversation a sense of flow. While I haven't used this exact process for research interviews, much of this method is applicable (although we wouldn't produce a compilation of research snippets; instead, we'd stop when we've identified the main themes or insights emerging from interviews).

Software tools certainly make it easier to convert raw data to insights. But ultimately, the most powerful use for note-taking during interviews is augmenting your ability to listen closely to the other person. For me, handwritten notes remain *the* essential capture method during interviews—whether in podcasts or during research sessions.

Typing vs. Writing Your Notes

Many people can type faster than they can write. Typed notes can easily be shared electronically, and no one has to read your handwriting or interpret your spelling errors. However, taking notes on a computer creates other challenges. Do you have sufficient battery power, or will you have to plug in? Can you type without clackety-clacking? What if you move around in the environment? Can you quickly move your laptop and still type on whatever surface is at hand? Can you continue to appear engaged even as you glance back and forth at the screen? Although this is also an issue when writing notes by hand, breaking eye contact to look at a screen can appear to be rude (as participants wonder if you are checking email), while the screen itself can be distracting for you.

Tablets and smartphones offer an alternative: although you won't be seen hiding behind the screen or lid, looking at a mobile device during the interview can be even more fraught with faux pas. It's not impossible to work around this issue, but simply showing up and using your smartphone as if you were in a meeting or waiting for your barista to finish your order isn't going to cut it. Throw in the lower typing speeds, and you're limited in what you can do with these.

It's a good bet that interviewers who use note-taking to help remember the interview are doing some kinesthetic learning; perhaps that effect isn't quite as strong when typing. If your goal is to juice your own memory, stick with writing. If you want roughs of the interview that can be shared (and you can keep your device interactions on the down-low), then type. And if you live for the moment, set it all aside and just focus on your interactions with your participant. Regardless, make sure that you are recording the entire interview using audio or video, as I discuss later in this chapter.

In her book *Mixed Methods*,[2] Sam Ladner encouraged user research notetakers to choose only the best moments for verbatim quotes, where there's emotion, or a unique way of expressing an idea. She also said to document paralinguistic information (e.g., hesitation and volume) and nonlinguistic information (e.g., gestures and facial expressions). Jorge Arango (in his book, *Duly Noted*[3]) suggests that

---

2 Sam Ladner, *Mixed Methods: A Short Guide to Applied Mixed Methods Research*, (self-pub., Amazon, 2019), www.mixedmethodsguide.com/

3 Jorge Arango, *Duly Noted: Principles and Practices for Thriving in the Information Age* (New York: Rosenfeld Media, 2023).

writing longhand can nudge a listener to take notes that capture the gist of the ideas, rather than surrendering to the temptation of transcribing.

> When taking notes, you should be descriptive, not interpretive. If Larry tells you he has worked 14 hours a day for the last 10 years, your notes should read "Worked 14 hrs/day for 10 years," not "Larry is a workaholic." If it's crucial to capture your interpretations, be sure to separate them from your observations, using capitalization or some other visual cue, such as "IS LARRY A WORKAHOLIC?" At this stage of rough notes, it's easy to lose track of what you were told versus the conclusions you made, so take care in how you document the two.

Audio Recording the Interview

An audio recording will capture all the verbal interactions between you and your participants. Of course, you can't see the demonstrations or exercises. Something like "I'd probably put this one with that one because they're kinda the same" might be hard to interpret later if you don't remember which items were being discussed. Although you can facilitate the discussion for the benefit of the audio recording (narrating what the participant is doing, like "So you would put the blue prototype in the same group as the orange prototype?"), it can feel unnatural. You shouldn't treat the documentation as more important than the interpersonal interaction.

Depending on the field environment, you can probably get away with a simple digital audio recorder. The growth of podcasting has created a market for high-quality devices. They are small and hold hours and hours of audio. Depending on how it handles noise cancellation, some background noise—especially clattering dishes and background music—can appear more prominent in the recording than you experienced it, so perform some tests. Be aware of how loud you and your participant will sound.

Based on what you plan to do with the recording, you may consider adding an external mic to your audio recorder; think about how having mics attached to the recorder will impact you and your participant being able to move around their environment. I don't recommend a body microphone (also called a *lavalier mic*) because everyone will have to be mic'd, and if a new participant joins spontaneously, you can't easily include them.

Beyond that, attaching a lavalier is a physically close act that needs to happen at the beginning of the interview. When your relationship with the participant is at its most vulnerable, they will need to—with your guidance—attach a small device to or under their clothing, near their face. This is a delicate interaction that doesn't seem necessary if you can otherwise be satisfied with the audio quality. Film production best practices are useful up to a point, but the needs of fieldwork are different.

And yes, I reluctantly concede[4] that you can use a recording app in your smartphone, but consider the privacy and ethics concerns that arise from storing this data on your personal device or on a business device that is connected online to social media and so on. More tactically, be sure that your phone has enough storage space for the recorded audio files and that your battery will last throughout the session. Test to see what happens if a call comes in. You might be able to use airplane mode to mitigate any problems, but will you remember to turn on airplane mode every time? Check how easily you can monitor the recording status of the app during the interview. There are few things more distressing to a researcher than realizing that your recording device has not actually been recording for the past half hour!

Transcribing Your Audio Files

As remote research has become widely used, researchers have taken advantage of the built-in transcription capabilities of video-calling platforms. While the technology continues to improve, these transcripts are still not good and often not even good enough. But because they are free (or included in the price) and convenient, they've become a standard. Some tools don't identify or separate the speakers, and they don't handle non-Western accents, technical language, or brand names. The result is something that is very hard to read and parse. This is too far from the detailed representation of the interview you need.

---

4   I am loathe to endorse a casual attitude of "Oh, I'll just use my phone" in case someone hasn't planned for some particular scenario, and thus is at a greater risk of losing the precious recording.

No doubt the quality will continue to improve, but ideally you should be using human-finished transcripts—whether a human does all of the transcription or does a correction pass on the auto-generated transcript. There are many transcription services that will take digital files and transcribe them. Most services can remove "ummm..." and other hesitations and repeated words. This is called a *clean verbatim transcript*. I prefer to have those bits and pieces included because they help make the transcription come alive, revealing the personality of the participant, as well as illustrating the thinking process that went into answering the questions. I think this sort of human metadata is helpful in interpretation and analysis.

Costs for transcription depend on factors like the total number of voices (how many interviewers and how many participants), accents, and turnaround time.

Some researchers prefer to do their own transcribing (perhaps those coming from social science where that was the norm), explaining that that close and painstaking revisiting of the interviews helps them begin their analysis and synthesis. Realistically, there are few professional environments where researchers have the time for this.

Video Recording the Interview

Video cameras are small, unobtrusive, and make for a viable default recording device. I take audio recorders as backup but rely on video in most situations. With a video camera, you can capture the specifics of what the participant means by, "That part right there is the best one to use," as long as someone actually moves the camera to capture those specifics. You also can capture body language and nuanced elements in the conversation, which, of course, is not possible with audio recordings.

Buy an inexpensive mini (or "tabletop") tripod. This will make it easier to set the camera down during stationary parts of the interview but will still allow you to easily grab it when you move around the environment. I haven't found that the presence of the camera is intimidating for people, but setting it and forgetting it helps to focus you on the participant and the interview, rather than on the camera. When you are holding the camera, be aware that, even when it's facing away from you, the microphone is much closer to your mouth than the participant's, so be sensitive to your interjections, snickers, and mm-hmms, as they will really pop on the audio and can overlap with good sound bites (Figure 8.1). For the novice interviewer, don't worry about moderating your rapport building for the camera, but for everyone else, it's worth keeping in mind, because it can be annoying or embarrassing when reviewing the recording.

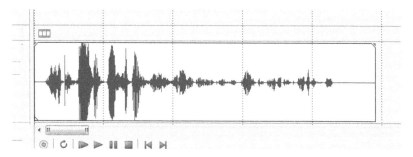

FIGURE 8.1

The interviewer's affirmations can be louder than the participant's comments.

NOTE DON'T RUN OUT OF JUICE!

Be sure to have enough batteries on hand to get through the interview. I've found that cameras ship with a fairly small battery, but larger-capacity batteries are available, including compatible ones from third-party manufacturers. Shop online and stock up.

Although some cameras can adjust for backlighting, you should generally avoid having your participants in front of a window; even if you can see them, they will probably just appear in silhouette on the video.

Be prepared to manage the large files you create. Even on the lowest-quality settings, over the course of a small study, you can end up with gigabytes of video without trying too hard. That much digital data can fill up drives and is almost impossible for mortals (those of us with non-Pixar quality infrastructure) to move around a network.

Even if you don't edit video into a specific deliverable, it's often the richest archival artifact of the fieldwork. Video also reassures your team that they can go back at any time to watch the interviews.

HOW TO GET VIDEO AS GOOD AS YOUR INSIGHTS

By Ted Frank

Ted Frank is a storyteller with Backstories Studio. He has been in marketing for over 30 years and in consumer insights and strategy for more than 20.

As a company that has created hundreds of videos for research and strategy firms, Backstories Studio has seen too many examples of stellar research work become unusable because of poor video or sound quality. And it breaks our hearts. What's more, for some clients, the video deliverable is often the only way they see your insights. So, it often becomes the way they evaluate you as well.

Here are some tips to get high-quality video, even if you have only five minutes to set up and have never been to film school:

- **Participant placement:** Where you place your participants is the biggest key to getting good quality. Pick a space that is quiet and bright enough to see the color of your participant's eyes. And unless it's important to the project, select a place where the background does not distract from your participant.

- **Light:** People tend to look best when light comes from the side and slightly in front of them (up to a 45° angle). A window works great in the daytime. Lights will work at night. Don't place your participants with the window behind them, or they will appear dark. Lights shining down will light them, but they will appear older because of the shadows those lights create. Lighting them from the front will also work, but they can end up looking like an episode of *Cops*, and if the light is in their eyes, it will make it difficult for them to see you. See Figure 8.2 for an optimal setup.

continues

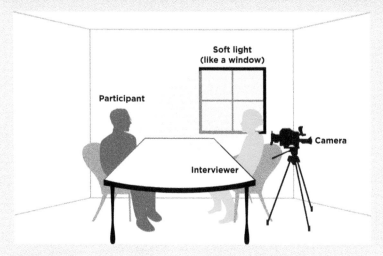

FIGURE 8.2
Position the camera and the people so that the participant is lit by soft angled light.

- **Sound:** In research, sound quality is often even more important than picture quality, especially if you're picking clips by what your participants say. Where you place your microphone is everything. It's just like real life: People sound intimate when they're close to you and can be hard to hear when they're across the street. Shotgun mics work well for groups if you can point them at the person speaking. Because that's difficult, though, a second mic in the center of the group will save you. A lot of researchers get scared when they see that some of these mics can cost $400. However, if you rely on your camera mic alone, you'll end up paying that same money in editing costs to reduce the room noise. And your clip will never sound as good as it would have if you had placed the mic closer to your participant to begin with. So, it's better to spend the money initially and let your work shine.

- **Setting up the camera:** Thankfully, cameras have gotten a lot better over the years. High-quality recording is a lot more affordable and will give your editor many more options for your final video. When setting up your camera, place it in front of your participant, with the interviewer in between it and the light or window (refer to Figure 8.2). It works best if the participant is framed a bit to one side and looking across the frame, toward the interviewer. When participants look directly into the camera, the setting appears staged.

Frame your picture up close if you want to capture emotion but leave room in case your subject shifts or sways (and they always do). That will also leave you room for a nametag if you choose to place one in your video. Finally, look again at your participant's eyes. If you can't see the color, move the light closer until you can.

Practice a few times before you get into the field, and you'll be able to set all this up in just a few minutes. You'll end up with an impressive video and a lot fewer hours and expenses down the line.

Photographing the Interview

Even if you're capturing imagery by using video, still pictures are essential. When you make the deliberate choice to point and shoot, you are building the story of your participant. Although the image in the camera is similar to a frame of video, that frame is packed in with all the other frames of video and requires effort for you to extract. You can return from the field with a set of photos and easily share an impromptu narrative of the interview by flipping through the photos on the camera. Even better, you will notice details in the photo that you didn't consciously perceive at the time. Video, with its audio track and its movement through time, doesn't afford that extra detail as easily. You might choose to just take still pictures and record audio and not bother recording video.

Be aware of how your picture taking will feel to the participants. Even though they agree to the use of photography when they sign your release, let the interview settle in before you start taking pictures. You can verbally confirm that it's okay before you take your first picture. If you are taking pictures of people, do it without the flash. If your second interviewer is taking pictures, they should not distract from the interview.

Be sure to prepare a shot list so that you have some ideas about which pictures you need to take.

Sketching the Interview

Sketching can be an appropriate medium when you can't take pictures. If you can't get an image of the participant's online banking screen, you can sketch the different regions of the interface and write callouts for some of their comments. Because they can see the sketch, they can be reassured that you aren't capturing private information and can clarify and correct your notes.

Caroline James takes that even further, using sketching as an active method to reflect back to her participants what she's hearing and to draw them out further (see Figure 8.3). She uses a combination of several specific techniques: visual recording, mind mapping, and visual note-taking (sometimes referred to as *sketchnoting*).[5] She sketches in

---

5   A great intro is at www.core77.com/posts/19678/sketchnotes-101-the-basics-of-visual-note-taking-19678; also check out Adam Menter's primer at https://portigal.com/visual

front of (and even with) her interview participants to engage them in creating a visual document of the interview.

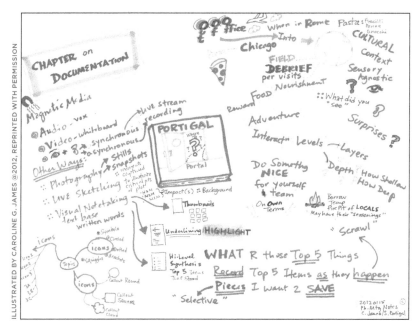

FIGURE 8.3
Caroline James took these notes while interviewing me about this chapter.

I worked in the field with designer Jorge Gordon. His technique for note-taking lay somewhere in between purely visual and purely textual; he used only words and lines but created a visual flow that captured his own experience (see Figure 8.4). As with many aspects of interviewing users, note-taking can be highly individualistic.

NOTE COLLECTING ARTIFACTS

You should collect tangible examples from your fieldwork experience—for example, buy an item from the company store, ask for a brochure, save your security pass, or keep the sample printout. These artifacts can go up on the wall in your analysis room, be passed around in meetings, or referred to later for inspiration, validation, or further insight.

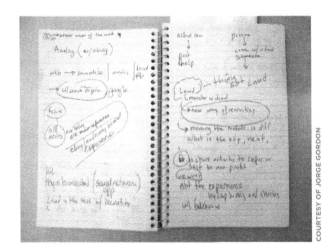

FIGURE 8.4
Jorge Gordon's field-
work notes include
both sketch and text
elements.

Debriefing After the Interview

When putting together your fieldwork schedule, you must absolutely
allow time for your field team to debrief after each interview. After
you leave the fieldwork site, go for food and drink and talk about the
interview. The longer you wait (say, until the next day or the next
week), the less you will remember, and the more jumbled up the
different interviews will become. For remote interviews, plan ahead
for debriefs by setting up separate calendar blocks that come immediately after each interview. Set the expectation that observers and
interviewers will join a new video call to debrief.

If you debrief as an open-ended conversation, make sure that someone takes notes and shares them with everyone. Otherwise, use a
debrief worksheet (see an example on next page[6]) to capture initial
thoughts, surprises, and changes for subsequent interviews. Ask,
"What would we design for *this* user?" Don't worry about being too
conclusive; this is a provocative way to start making sense of the
interview. You aren't making design decisions; this is hypothetical,
speculative, and easily discarded when future data takes you in a
different direction. Make sure that your fellow researchers understand that hypothesizing conclusions is a creative exercise.

---

6   This worksheet (and an additional example) is available as a PDF at
    https://portigal.com/debrief

If you are running an interview on your own, complete a debrief worksheet anyway. Ask a colleague to review each day's worksheets with you.

Project *Name* Debrief

Participant: _____ **Researchers:** _____

Fill this out immediately after the interview, together with both interviewers. This document will serve as the key resources for the collaborative fieldwork debriefing and analysis, so please be thoughtful and thorough.

GETTING TO KNOW YOU—*Describe*

Describe the person you spoke to. What do they do? What are they into? What is their home environment like?

_____

_____

How did they describe their process of getting the PRODUCT?

_____

_____

LIFE WITH PRODUCT

How are they using the PRODUCT? What features are they using? What does this device mean to them?

_____

_____

What kinds of accessories do they use? Which ones aren't they using? Why?

_____

_____

What do they like most about the PRODUCT? How is it best serving their needs?

_____

_____

continues

Project *Name* Debrief (continued)

What challenges have they had? What are some of their unmet needs and wishes?

_____

_____

What surprised them? What surprised you?

_____

_____

PROTOTYPE—Assess

What did they like about the PROTOTYPE? What are the features and benefits that appealed most to them? What didn't they like? (Use + and − here to make a bulleted list of answers.)

_____

_____

How did they imagine using it in their current use cases? What new use cases did they imagine?

_____

_____

What feedback did they have about **usability, audio, price**, etc.? What **suggestions** did they make?

_____

_____

Surprises or Aha! moments from this interview? New thinking? Connections to other interviews?

_____

_____

Insights about the interview process? What would you ask, or ask differently in the next interview? Any advice for the team?

_____

_____

Writing Field Notes

Many researchers sit down shortly after the interview and write up notes in some detail, using their notes, memory, and recordings. These field notes can easily run several pages long and emphasize narrative and description over conclusions or business implications. It's a time-consuming task and something I've stopped doing, especially since I began using transcripts. For trained social scientists, this is likely part of their training and an essential part of their process. Although writing notes is undoubtedly valuable, you should consider whether or not you have time in your schedule to do this.

Sharing Field Highlights

As soon as possible after an interview—ideally before the next interview begins—I rapidly write a top-of-mind version of the session. I am not trying to capture all the details, nor I am identifying patterns or making recommendations. Rather, I am creating a lightweight, sharable story that brings a bit of the flavor of the fieldwork (through real details about real people) to the broader team. With practice, this story will take only a few minutes to write and share. It can be emailed or posted into a Slack thread or otherwise posted where the broader team can read it.

To manage expectations, I'll preface the first one with some context.

> We like to share brief anecdotes from each interview during fieldwork. These aren't field notes and aren't intended to capture everything that happened in the session—rather, they are just a few quick stories to give a sense of each session and what we're seeing. We will have transcripts which have all the details.
>
> We like to share with the team—especially everyone who is participating in the fieldwork—and hope that the notes will trigger discussion and further sharing of stories, ideas, questions, etc. We'll post them here each day, but if you see an opportunity to share more broadly, please go for it!

Here's a (lightly redacted) example from a project.

Alex: Alex heads up APAC recruiting. He's been with Mango-Tech for 5 years and recalls the time when he joined as "The Wild West" when there were only 80 people and no process; now at 500 people, it's a 180-degree change to a mature organization. His #1 priority is quality of hire, and he's been involved in a training program aimed at hiring managers that give them a robust and repeatable process for interviewing for competency. They are working on a new process where people provide detailed feedback within 24 hours of an interview. Feedback to a candidate is key to the candidate experience. But nowadays, if someone has a good interview experience, it's going to simply be the result of someone going "above and beyond." His group has faced a challenge in hiring against attrition and has started to set hiring targets that include an estimate, based on previous quarters, of likely attrition. Culturally, this move away from hiring people they've worked with elsewhere is raising some eyebrows as to whether or not that will apply to the group of prospects now joining MangoTech. His future vision includes more automation, where many of today's processes are needlessly manual, like assembling a package about a candidate in [software tool].

Not only are these field highlights quick to create, but they are also quick to read, so it's an easy way to keep people involved without placing too high a demand on their time. I've been surprised at how excited some teams can be about the research just through this low effort. Despite all the pressure on research to be specific and actionable, these bite-sized pieces can really be well-received and valuable.

The Last Word

By documenting the interview, you are capturing a definitive detailed record of the interview. It's also a way for you to process and remember the insights and takeaways that come to you while the interview is happening.

- You can't catch everything by taking notes, but you absolutely need to get *everything*. In the moment, you will miss details, mishear a word, or not fully grasp the context.
- Recording audio or video is the only way to capture all the details of your interview.
- If you take notes on a computer or other device, can you do so silently and maintain your engaged eye contact with the participant?
- Notes should be descriptive rather than interpretive; when you go back to them later, it's hard to tell the difference between what actually happened and your own interpretations.
- Use a small video camera with a pocket tripod or a simple digital audio recorder; external mics will improve audio quality, but body mics create an awkward interaction with the participant when setting up.
- Have plenty of batteries for all of your devices and be aware of how long they should last.
- Take lots of pictures; they often reveal something different later on.
- Sit down with the field team right after the interview and debrief about key takeaways. Soon after, write up quick highlights and share them with the rest of your team.

Making Sense of Your Data

There's a naïve approach to interviewing users, as I mentioned in Chapter 1, "Interviewing Addresses a Business Need," where the whole exercise is seen as making the effort to speak with users and learn some fairly straightforward things—usually what people do and don't like about the product as it is today. The team then tallies the specific feedback and decides what they are going to fix or build.

Over the last eight chapters, we've considered how to run interviews so that you get more specific, nuanced, and richer information. Making sense of those interviews is harder than totaling points of feedback. Still, it's not uncommon for teams to essentially debrief and summarize after research and consider themselves done. Getting the most value out of doing research can be very time consuming—some people plan for two to three hours of analysis and synthesis for every hour they spend doing research. But the more time you put in, the more you'll get out.

You want to make sure that data becomes insights, and insights become opportunities—for new products, features, services, designs, and strategies, but also new opportunities for teams to embrace a user-centered approach to their work. In this chapter, we'll look at the process for doing that.

Analysis and Synthesis

Colloquially, researchers tend to use these words, *analysis* and *synthesis*, interchangeably to refer to the entire process of making sense of research data, but they refer to two different, yet tightly integrated, activities.

Analysis (Figure 9.1) refers to breaking larger pieces into smaller ones in order to extract meaning (for example, interviews and transcripts into anecdotes and stories). *Synthesis* (Figure 9.2) means combining multiple pieces into something new (for example, building themes, implications, and opportunities).

This isn't to suggest that first you do analysis and, once you are completely finished, move onto synthesis. Your brain will helpfully mix them up a bit. Once you've done a little bit of analysis, having pulled some smaller elements out of all that data, you'll probably start thinking about this data in a new way, playing with possible ways to recombine those elements into new, richer insights. Doing a little bit of synthesis doesn't mean that you are jumping ahead too quickly; it just means that you have an active and curious mind, and you are exploring possibilities with what you're learning. The key is being clear to yourself when you are being creative with your data by playing with possibilities and when you are formally synthesizing.

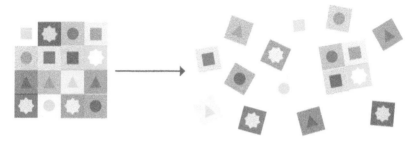

FIGURE 9.1
Analysis is breaking larger pieces into smaller ones in order to extract meaning.

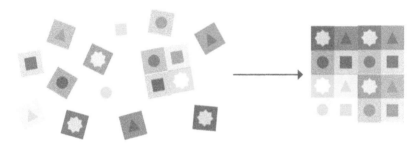

FIGURE 9.2
Synthesis is combining multiple pieces into something new.

Some exciting news: You've already started analyzing! Some of the important activities that take place during fieldwork (debriefing and sharing field highlights as described in Chapter 8, "Document-ing the Interview") are the first steps in analysis. You're taking the experience of an entire interview and breaking it down into smaller chunks—that's analysis! As you move through a research project, analysis (and eventually synthesis) move from a background activity to one that you are deliberately focusing on.

Write a Topline Report

After you've wrapped up all your interviews, you should compile a starter set of 5 to 15 thematic topics that have probably come up in your debrief conversations and field highlights. At this stage, you shouldn't be digging into transcripts and recordings, but rather the analysis you've already done. You're really just processing the experience of being in the field by documenting what's come up so far. You can also add in topics that you think will be relevant, although you may not be exactly sure what the specifics are. Identify interesting areas and provocative questions, such as, "There seems to be a relationship between people's comfort with making mistakes and their choice between different companies' products" (for example). You don't need to know what the relationship actually is at this point; instead, you are just noting patterns and weak signals (a term from electrical engineering that has been adopted by futurists) that you see.

This set of emerging themes and early findings becomes a *topline report.* In the introduction to the topline reports I write, I include the following:

> This topline is based on early impressions, not a formal analysis of our data. This is a chance for us to share stories and initial insights from the fieldwork and to discuss what jumped out at us and list questions we still have.

This standard paragraph helps set expectations for the rest of the team. Sometimes researchers are concerned that their colleagues will take early findings and dash off to implementation, so it's important to clarify where you are in the process. You can include key milestones from the overall project calendar, point to what is coming next and indicate how future deliverables will be different than what's in the topline (and when they can expect them).

You should create topline reports in Microsoft Word or Google Docs. It's more formal than an email, but less formal than a slide deck. Don't include graphics, fieldwork photos, logos, or other visual elements that are often found in slide decks. You want to match the formality of this document to the project milestone—the conclusion of full-on fieldwork and the transition into full-on analysis and synthesis. You don't want any of this content to be misinterpreted as more conclusive or actionable than is warranted.

Make sure that you go through the topline report together and listen for the team's concerns, skepticism, excitement, and curiosity.

The topline helps get the rest of the team on board with where the research is heading, but it also gives you some perspective on what kind of reactions you will encounter. If something excites them, make sure that you look into it more in your in-depth analysis and synthesis and see if there's anything more to say about it. If you encounter resistance, make sure that you build your case persuasively through the rest of the process.

Analysis: Tagging Your Data

After the topline report comes the more formal data processing stages, where you will uncover significant new insights that go well beyond the topline. Get your data in text form, like transcripts, and divide them among the team. This typically includes everyone who went in the field, although I don't recommend asking people who weren't involved in the fieldwork to review transcripts, especially people who aren't researchers. Don't spread the data too thinly; people do best if they have at least two or three interviews to work with. Make sure that each interview has been assigned to a team member.

Each team member should go through their set of transcripts quickly and tag them. By tagging (also called *coding*), you are noting which aspects of the session are interesting to you, and what it is you find interesting about them. And to be clear, you're going back to the actual interview itself, not your notes or interpretations or summaries.

There are a variety of tagging styles,[1] but the most useful difference is between *open* versus *closed* tagging. In open tagging, there's no specific set of codes, you just go through and describe the individual elements as best suits. In closed tagging, you begin with a defined set of tags, and each time you note something interesting, you use one of those tags, or you define a new tag at that point (see Figure 9.3). Open tagging runs the risk of being wildly inconsistent and divergent whereas closed tagging limits what kind of things you can extract. Whether those limitations help or hinder your work depends on the nature of your research objective and also your own style. Some people (like me) can't handle closed tagging; I find it just too constraining.

---

1 Find a detailed breakdown of coding in Delve, "The Essential Guide to Coding Qualitative Data," https://delvetool.com/guide/#qualitativecoding; also Johnny Saldaña, *The Coding Manual for Qualitative Researchers* (Thousand Oaks, CA: Sage, 2021).

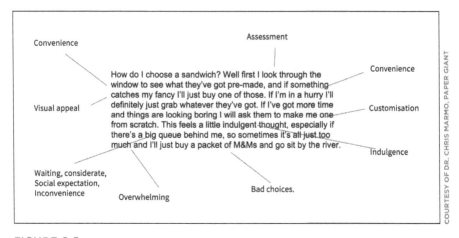

Convenience

Assessment

Convenience

Visual appeal

How do I choose a sandwich? Well first I look through the window to see what they've got pre-made, and if something catches my fancy I'll just buy one of those. If I'm in a hurry I'll definitely just grab whatever they've got. If I've got more time and things are looking boring I will ask them to make me one from scratch. This feels a little indulgent though, especially if there's a big queue behind me, so sometimes it's all just too much and I'll just buy a packet of M&Ms and go sit by the river.

Customisation

Indulgence

Waiting, considerate,
Social expectation,
Inconvenience

Overwhelming

Bad choices.

COURTESY OF DR. CHRIS MARMO, PAPER GIANT

FIGURE 9.3

In this representation of (probably closed) tagging, elements of the participant's narrative are marked with the themes, principles, and attitudes they reveal.

There are quite a few tools for tagging, some of which are better suited to either open or closed tagging. I've long preferred to do my open tagging on paper, sitting with a stack of printed transcripts and a pen, circling and scrawling comments and short marginal notes that summarize, pose questions, note an emergent pattern, flag great stories and key quotes, label, and so on (Figure 9.4). These can be in the form of labels ("This is another example of BLURRING BOUND-ARIES"), questions ("Where did she get this process?"), or of need ("They'd really benefit from an all-in-one bundle here!").

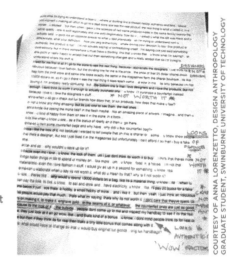

FIGURE 9.4

An interview transcript is marked up by hand showing annotations and tags.

COURTESY OF ANNA LORENZETTO, DESIGN ANTHROPOLOGY
GRADUATE STUDENT, SWINBURNE UNIVERSITY OF TECHNOLOGY

I like the physical aspect of actually writing by hand, adding emphasis and flourish that captures my energy and excitement. This is messier and less efficient than typed text, which could be copied or exported, but access to a printer is less common than it used to be.

You can also use Microsoft Word or Google Docs to do open tagging (Figure 9.5). You should use the commenting feature so there's a clear distinction between what was said in the interview and your observations. If you must put your tags into the text itself, use a different color or typeface to preserve that distinction.

FIGURE 9.5

An interview transcript is marked-up in Google Docs showing annotations and tags.

For decades, academics in social science have been using computer-assisted qualitative data analysis software (or CAQDAS) tools, such as NVivo, MAXQDA, and ATLAS.ti, to do open and closed tagging. More recently, there are quite a few tools aimed at the professional user experience researcher (see the discussion of tools for research in Chapter 2, "Research Logistics").

The transcript of a two-hour interview might run 35 pages, and with a bit of practice in skimming and annotating, you can get through it in under an hour. This activity is primarily analysis, but there's going to be some synthesis in there as well. But where possible, limit the amount of solution generating you do in this stage; you're mostly trying to describe and characterize what you've learned about this person.

By Shima Houshyar

Shima Houshyar is a NYC-based freelance UX Researcher with a graduate degree in anthropology.

In both the social sciences and UX research, coding qualitative data is mostly similar, but is aimed toward different goals. In the social sciences, especially anthropology, the length of fieldwork often generates large amounts of data—field notes, journals, memos, interviews, and observations. In order to dive deeply into this analysis, a slower iterative process of analysis, synthesis, writing, and rewriting is required. By contrast, in UX research, the analytical process tends to move quicker but in more iterative cycles of research and analysis.

One of the challenges of anthropological research is the tendency to see data "everywhere" and "nowhere" due to the total immersion in one's research site. Anthropologists typically spend between 12 to 24 months in their research sites, and some may return to the same place many times throughout their careers. This results in a massive amount of data. How do you know which pieces of data are important and which aren't? In anthropology, this tends to be an iterative process as we look at data from interviews or observations from later in the research and compare it with data collected earlier on. The anthropologist may not have the full context of what they are observing or hearing from their participants in the earlier stages, when they are new to the field. As time goes on and the anthropologist continues to engage with their research subjects' lives, a certain focus might start to emerge in the kinds of things they look for. Coding the data and writing frequent memos that document initial findings and hypotheses are important tools for generating and organizing your insights in a systematic manner.

In my anthropological work, the first step in analyzing qualitative data is inductive (or bottom-up) coding, meaning that I first "let the data speak to me"—reading over notes and transcripts with an open mind—so I can see patterns and relevant categories emerge. I then start annotating the notes and transcripts with codes that are themes from my observations or interviews. As I am coding my data, I write short memos for myself to quickly capture some insights, such as what I think might be happening or what the relationship is between the different things that I've been observing. I take those themes and organize them into larger categories in a separate document (a kind of affinity diagramming, although academics don't use that term), and write a preliminary analysis of what the connections between those themes might be, to see if any larger categories jump out at me. Those larger categories become a preliminary analysis or theory. Comparing the codes across different moments of my research helps me identify the most important or relevant pieces of data. This is when research insights start to congeal and solidify, and I start to acquire a picture of what is happening and what I may want to write about. Oftentimes, the analysis that emerges from my codes and categories actually ends up pointing me in new and unanticipated directions, and I will walk away from the field with a different research question than the one with which I entered the field.

The coding process is somewhat similar in UX research, but applied with a different scope, where we're less amenable to significant changes in the research question. The kinds of research questions one can ask in an industry setting are oftentimes delimited by other factors such as business goals, stakeholder needs, limited budget, and tight timelines. The type of analysis that one does as a UX researcher varies from project to project. For example, for generative user interviews, I might follow a two-step approach to analyzing qualitative data. First, I conduct bottom-up (or inductive) coding similar to what I described for academic research, to see what patterns, themes, or categories emerge. To speed up the process, I simultaneously layer an additional set of systematized top-down tags over my bottom-up codes. For example, if my initial bottom-up code is about "taking too much time" to complete a task, I might add the top-down tag "pain points" to indicate that overly time-consuming workflows are a pain point for the user. Or I might tag a section "tools" to indicate what tools the participant is currently using to solve their problems. Tags such as "pain points" and "tools" are top-down and kept consistent across participants. Tags such as "taking too much time" are bottom-up and originate in a specific participant transcript.

I then take this analysis and move on to synthesis, detecting larger themes or categories. Through affinity diagramming, I quickly map relationships between what people are feeling, saying, or experiencing and the product, feature, or process that I'm investigating. These quick insights can then be easily shared with stakeholders. Similarly, to academic research, UX research also follows an iterative process but on a much quicker cycle. Oftentimes, we may not have enough time to truly dig into our data, but our coded analysis should help us establish some assumptions that we can test in the next round of research. We then cross out those assumptions or solutions that don't hold up to our analysis and move on to other feature or product opportunities to explore.

Ultimately, there is no single right way to analyze qualitative data, and there are significant overlaps between social scientific research analysis in academia and in an industry setting.

Synthesis: Collaboration and Clustering

After the team has finished tagging the transcripts, the group should then reconvene for a synchronous workshop activity. Structure your session so that each coded transcript is presented (by whoever did the coding) back to the group, essentially as a case study. You can give a bit of background about the individual, and then page through your tags and pick out the most interesting ones to share. Discuss each topic briefly and then create a sticky note that summarizes the key point of that thing. (You can designate someone to be the "scribe" who captures that sticky, or people can each write their own.) Annotate each sticky with the source (such as the interviewee name or initials).

Presenting the first few interviews to the group will take a very long time because everything is new, and everything is interesting. By the time you get to the end, you'll be moving much more quickly. Plan for a series of three- or four-hour sessions and expect to average about an hour per interview (see Figure 9.6).

FIGURE 9.6

In analysis/synthesis sessions, stories and examples from transcripts and other data are synthesized into key findings, takeaways, and opportunities.

Of course, you can do this with a digital whiteboard, whether or not you are running a remote session. In theory, a digital whiteboard is easier to archive (although digital files do tend to accumulate), and some tools will import and export tags and other data to and from other programs. If, like me, you prefer marking up transcripts with a pen, you may also prefer the tactile quality of working with stickies in the real world.

At the end of a case study presentation, put all the stickies up on the whiteboard (unless you've been doing it as you go). You can use these breaks to revisit how you are categorizing the stickies. You may want to start with the headings from your topline as initial categories. You can use a different size and color sticky for category labels and put those headings up before you even start going through transcripts. Or, as you proceed, use an ad hoc organizing scheme like "all things related to shopping" or "what people are doing" or "what people are feeling" or "pain points" (see Figure 9.7). After completing a couple of interviews, take time between each presentation to review your grouping and categorization, looking for more meaningful ways of connecting different elements together (see Figure 9.8). As you assemble those groupings, you will collectively begin to develop a new, shared point of view that goes beyond the mere findings. This process—often called *affinity mapping*—works best when people are thinking and talking together.

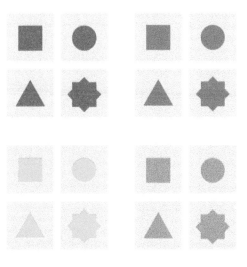

FIGURE 9.7
Be opportunistic with your initial grouping scheme, using whatever makes sense at first.

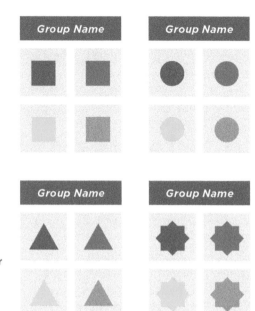

FIGURE 9.8
Thoughtfully regroup your elements and label the groups to capture your point of view.

NOTE KNOWING ALONE

I describe analysis and synthesis as a team effort. Ideally, that's true, but realistically it's not always possible. Maybe there are other people doing research, but they are focused on other work, or maybe you're the only one. On your own, the process is the same, although you might use the tools differently. When working alone, I prefer to use a word processor and type and cut-and-paste. Other people like to work with actual sticky notes, or a digital whiteboard. Fundamentally, it's still the same work. Even if you can't share the whole process with a teammate, find some trusted people who you can pull in from time-to-time to give a quick run-down. Talking through your ideas to someone else will help you shape them, and their feedback can help you see where your thinking isn't fully clear or believable.

Delivering Research Results

There will be more opportunities for synthesis as you transform your results into some form of output or deliverable. How you summarize and communicate the results of your analysis and synthesis will depend on the project objectives and the communication norms for your team and organization. Researchers create reports, decks, and email summaries that get shared over email and online collaboration platforms and presented at meetings and lunchtime seminars.

In Chapter 1, "Interviewing Addresses a Business Need," we looked at interviewing your stakeholders as a way to help understand the business problem and the research question. You also heard things in those interviews about what kind of results they expected, their concerns about where projects might lead, and maybe some guidance for communicating information. This is the point in the project to revisit those interviews and make use of what you learned.

There are some "standard" forms of interpreting and visualizing research that come in and out of vogue, such as personas[2] and journey maps. These may be effective forms, but you should choose the right way to communicate based on the goals, not by default.

You should have a way to help your colleagues see beyond their "so what?" reaction. The content of your report should be interesting, but it should also help people see the implications.

If your finding is "Customers aren't clear on the differences between our three service tiers," it can be helpful to be more explicit and add "We should help customers understand the differences between our service tiers." Depending on the context, it may not be appropriate to make a recommendation like "Give the service tiers names that reflect their ascending price point." You should be explicit (we found this problem *and we should address it*), but not necessarily specific, because it's possible that you don't know all the ways that this issue could be addressed, let alone what the best option might be.

In fact, the opportunity "We should help customers understand the differences between our service tiers" gets restated very nicely as a brainstorming question "How might we help our customers understand the differences between our service tiers?"

NOTE HOW MIGHT WE?

The prompt *how might we* (sometimes abbreviated as HMW) dates back to 1971[3] and has become a common phrase in UX and design thinking. Its value as a prompt is that it asks about pos-

---

2   While my position has slightly softened since then, I came out against personas many years ago in Steve Portigal, "Persona Non Grata," *Interactions* 15, no. 1 (2008): 72–73.

3   For a bit of history see Bob Basadur, "The Origin of How Might We," *Basadur* (blog), July 26, 2021, www.basadur.com/the-origin-of-how-might-we/

sibilities; it's not how *will* we, or how *should* we. It also uses an inclusive pronoun, *we*, to invite everyone in the conversation to consider what those possibilities are.

Brainstorming and Taking Action

You should ideally share your research findings in a presentation-style session and then convene a separate workshop-style session in which you brainstorm responses to the "How might we" questions. In the first setting, people are listening, as a group, to new information that challenges the status quo, and in the second setting, they are creating divergent ideas collaboratively. The different types of participation require different contexts, facilitation, and mindsets.

NOTE CONNECTING THE DOTS

Usually, people have been in brainstorming sessions before, and they may have even brainstormed how to address the business problem you started with. But what makes this session different is that they aren't being asked to just come up with stuff. Rather, you are helping them connect their ideas for solutions to what you learned in doing research. That's often new, or at least rare, for people.

For example, we had a team focused on community development, and the research led us to ask, "How might we foster lightweight interactions between people living in the same building?" Some of the ideas we brainstormed included giving free rent to someone who would serve as a "social concierge," putting parklets near the entrances, buying a shared commercial-sized refrigerator, giving group-purchase deals for local businesses, allowing meeting spaces in the lobby, and having a resource-exchange wall.

The goal of this workshop is to generate many ideas and not dismiss any of them. Resist the typical ways that ideas get dismissed. You want ideas that are beyond the purview of your team (try for packaging, services, retail, technology, acquisitions, legislative, media...anything), ideas that already exist elsewhere, and even bad ideas.[4] For one thing, bad ideas may not be that bad after all. (Sometimes as a constraint to a

---

4   My talk "The Power of Bad Ideas" has a lot more about this:
    https://vimeo.com/174801774

situation that you presume applies, you'll find that actually it does not apply.) Or you may prompt a fellow brainstormer to come up with a variation that is, in fact, a good idea.

Wrap up by reviewing the ideas together; you can do a dot-voting[5] activity to get a sense of what has excited the team. Organize a separate activity with a smaller group to sort and prioritize, according to the criteria that are most relevant to your team (say, strategic fit, feasibility, differentiation from competitors, and so on). Don't leave that session without assigning the next steps.

The Last Word

The emphasis here has been on gathering data in the field, but obviously you are doing that in order to do something with it: to unpack insights and turn them into opportunities for your teams to design new and better products and services. You also want to inform and inspire the organization with a richer and more nuanced perspective about the people you are serving.

- Working with research data is a combination of *analysis* (breaking larger pieces into smaller ones) and *synthesis* (combining multiple pieces into something new).

- From the experience you've had conducting the interviews, organize your initial takeaways into a topline report.

- Use the topline report to get early feedback from your team about what the research is starting to reveal. Uncover what insights may be challenging to accept and which ones are exciting. Use this intelligence to guide your deeper analysis.

- Divide up your transcripts among team members. Review interviews and tag transcripts to highlight insights, patterns, and quotes. Get the team back together and present interviews as case studies. Capture main points on sticky notes. Cluster stickies and write up your report.

- Brainstorm possible actions that the research insights might lead to, and then sort and prioritize the next steps you and your team will take.

---

5   An overview of this method is at https://en.wikipedia.org/wiki/Dot-voting

Making an Impact with Your Research

There comes a point for most user researchers (as well as for PwDR) where they realize that great research—well-planned, well-executed, well-analyzed, well-synthesized, and well-documented—doesn't automatically have the intended impact. They realize that they have to do more work to help their team leverage the most value from the research they've already done. Research leader Jerome Axle Brown tells the members of his team that they should plan to spend 50 percent of their time socializing completed research.

In this chapter, we'll consider ways that you can have more impact with your research. It's important to be aware that you are often tasked with changing people's minds in a busy, fast-paced environment where the people you want to influence didn't ask to have their minds changed, they don't expect to have their minds changed, and they may have very little incentive (in some cases actually a *disincentive*) to change their minds. There's no magic spell that will solve all the challenges you face. But the practices in this chapter should ground you in the basics and set you up to be creative and persistent in how you work with the rest of your organization.

TABLE 10.1 RESEARCH FINDINGS AND RECOMMENDATIONS TRACKER

Finding	Assigned To	Severity	Status
[Describe the finding—How many participants? What was the task they were trying to complete? What was the functionality that affected the completion of this task? Is there a suggestion if they had one, etc.? Do not include a possible solution—it will go into the Recommendation column.]	[Populate with names of your team]	High	Not Started

Planning and Tracking Research

One factor in having impact is ensuring that the research being done is relevant. As time passes, and teams grow or people come and go, an organization accumulates more and more research, including reports, raw data, notes, and other artifacts. This abundance of data creates challenges for planning, whether it's a research team identifying what research they see as needed or a PwDR responding to requests from stakeholders. How can people in the organization see what research has been done? This is a specific knowledge management problem where the solutions are referred to as *research repositories,* with the goals of extracting more value out of the research that has already been done and informing plans for future research.[1]

Let's look at some examples of how researchers in different organizations offer visibility into past and future research. You'll see elements of related needs, like having access to "What research has been done?" "What research is being planned?" "What data do we have?" "What questions do we have?" and "What impact have we had?" among others. At Salesforce, they created a rudimentary spreadsheet-based tracker to document research findings and recommendations (see Table 10.1).[2] This tracker provides a view across research projects of what has been learned and also suggests recommended product changes.

Recommendation	Solution	Affected Area	Affected Step	Comments
[Formulate your recommendation based on your knowledge of the related user personas and their JTBDs, your expertise, understanding of the product, and project requirements.]	[Document the solution that team agreed upon and how it relates to your recommendation.]	[Populate with what is appropriate: parts of the app, area of the screen.]	[Delete if don't need.]	

---

1   Jake Burghardt has been exploring repositories and related topics in articles at www.integratingresearch.com and in Jake Burghardt, *Stop Wasting Research* (New York: Rosenfeld Media, to be published 2024).

2   Anna Poznyakov and Richa Prajapati, "Get the Most Out of Stakeholder Collaboration—and Maximize Your Research Impact," *Medium*, February 17, 2021.

At another organization, Allana Wooley, a lead researcher, created a landing page in SharePoint where her colleagues could see user research deliverables like personas, journey maps, service blueprints, as well as research reports organized by the company's market segments. To help with planning future research, there's a section listing current and upcoming research efforts, as well as which teams are involved with and asking for that research.

And at yet another company, Justin Threlkeld, a research leader, took a different approach and built a shared board specifically for researchers to use. The board captured open research questions and research questions that had already been addressed (see Figure 10.1).

FIGURE 10.1

This board was designed for researchers to share different types of questions that they had previously addressed or that they hoped to address in the future.

Be proactive in identifying opportunities to learn about users. Instead of waiting for requests (which will be more tactical than strategic), be on the lookout for design questions and business objectives, and then propose research that aligns with expected business needs and may even serve multiple teams and initiatives.

For example, when Laith Ulaby was the Head of Research at Udemy, his team would propose upcoming research each quarter. He said,

"As the product teams were putting together *their* quarterly OKRs (Objectives and Key Results[3]), researchers were also evaluating what the research asks would be over the next quarter. The researchers then put that all together and came up with a proposal. We then did a readout of these plans to leadership."[4] Frances Karandy, formerly a research manager at Citrix, would take a longer view, planning out an entire year and developing research plans that aligned with scheduled product milestones and release plans. By being proactive, she also ensured that her team would cover research that was related to those product releases, as well as broader themes and bigger topics that would inform a greater swath of organizational decisions.[5]

NOTE UNDERSTANDING YOUR RESEARCH
REPOSITORY NEED

Before building or buying a software solution for a user research repository, you need to consider the specifics of your needs clearly. Answer these questions in order to focus on what problems you are hoping to solve:

- What is the current role of organizational knowledge?
- Who has the data and other info obtained from research?
- Who will add info to the repository?
- What types of data will they be adding?
- Who will maintain the info in the repository?
- Who needs the info from research?
- How will information be accessed?
  - Self-serve?
  - Via reference librarian?
- How will information be used?
  - Review before a study?
  - Review findings that haven't been acted on?
- What should be stored?
  - Data?
  - Insights?
  - Interpretations/conclusions?

3   "OKR," Wikipedia, Wikimedia Foundation, https://en.wikipedia.org/wiki/OKR

4   Steve Portigal, "30: Laith Ulaby of Udemy," *Dollars to Donuts* (podcast), April 3, 2020, https://portigal.com/podcast/30-laith-ulaby-of-udemy/

5   Steve Portigal, "3: Frances Karandy of Citrix," *Dollars to Donuts* (podcast), January 21, 2015, https://portigal.com/podcast/3-frances-karandy-of-citrix/

Prioritizing Your Limited Resources

Research teams frequently end up with more work than they can handle. Kate Lawrence, when she was Vice President of User Research at EBSCO Information Services, actively worked to reach that state, in order to promote a nascent function that not everyone was aware of or understood. "I did every single project that came my way. I said yes to everything just to get the demand, so that I could get the resources."[6] In corporate life, you don't get the resources unless you can show the demand, so she made sure her team would support any project to build awareness, goodwill, and with that demand, eventually more resources. Kate made a prioritization decision based on her desired outcome—not for the project or team product, but for the research practice itself.

In less extreme circumstances, even if you plan research a quarter or a year ahead of time, you will mitigate some amount of being overwhelmed with demand, but you will likely receive unexpected requests regardless. When Aviva Rosenstein was managing research at DocuSign, she would prioritize by working only with "the teams that...commit to acting on the research insights that we deliver. If they just want us to do a study to prove that they're right, then we don't have to take that project." If the only research being done is always applied, this really highlights the value of research.

Depending on how research requests come to you, you should create a standardized request template (see the template on next page). This doesn't necessarily mean forcing people to complete the form, but some teams use a worksheet as a way to facilitate a conversation with a stakeholder. You may be able to help that stakeholder by sharing research that has already been conducted. Sometimes the issue under consideration is one that could be addressed in another way, besides research. Otherwise, this information can help clarify the business problem and research question. (See Chapter 1, "Interviewing Addresses a Business Need.")

---

6 Steve Portigal, "13: Kate Lawrence of EBSCO," *Dollars to Donuts* (podcast), April 25, 2016, https://portigal.com/podcast/13-kate-lawrence-of-ebsco/

Research Request

Date: _____ Requester: _____ Team: _____

When do you need results from this research?

_____

_____

_____

_____

_____

Why do you need to do this research?

_____

_____

_____

_____

_____

What action will you take as a result of the research?

_____

_____

_____

_____

_____

What other data do you have already?

_____

_____

_____

_____

_____

_____

Researchers at Salesforce segmented their stakeholders[7] in order to prioritize whom to focus on (Figure 10.2). They considered two subjective attributes: how interested each stakeholder was in research, and how much influence they had in the organization. This framework produced four different segments, and they chose different strategies for each one. Rather than trying to change the entire organization, they focused their limited resources where they would have the most impact.

FIGURE 10.2

Researchers at Salesforce created this segmentation model of their stakeholders that helped them prioritize how they spent their time.

In setting up a research practice at Asurion, Lena Blackstock and Justin Threlkeld experimented with a hierarchy that prioritized how they would engage with research requests and project teams. The tiers were the following:

- Ignore (often low-risk, low-impact efforts)
- Passively support (providing feedback on project team's documents)

---

7   Anna Poznyakov and Richa Prajapati, "Get the Most Out of Stakeholder Collaboration—and Maximize Your Research Impact," *Medium*, February 17, 2021.

- Actively support (collaborating with the project team to plan and execute the work, say by recruiting users or writing an interview guide)
- Embed (someone from research became a member of the project team for a specific duration)
- Own (a project initiated or led by the research team, like a foundational study to develop behavioral personas)

> **NOTE** IMPACTFUL PRACTICES IN INDIVIDUAL RESEARCH PROGRAMS
>
> While this chapter emphasizes systemic and structural ways to approach user research, note that we've already covered multiple ways that you can operate individual research programs to have more impact.
>
> Chapter 1, "Interviewing Addresses a Business Need," highlighted best practices for maximizing the impact of individual user research efforts during the planning process, like establishing the business problem and research question and leading a Questions Workshop.
>
> Chapter 4, "The Successful Fieldwork Experience," looked at ways to engage colleagues in the interviews, by participating, debriefing, and reviewing highlights.
>
> Chapter 9, "Making Sense of Your Data," considered how members of the organization could be involved in the analysis and synthesis activities, from the topline through reading transcripts and identifying patterns and themes.

Delivery for Impact

In Chapter 9, we talked about different formats for deliverables. You have many options, but you can also take a strategic approach above and beyond choosing among those options. You can learn about your stakeholders and what type of communication will best impact them (say, a visual learner versus someone who responds to stories). Research leader Amanda Rosenburg doesn't have a one-size-fits-all approach to sharing research. She strives for a middle-ground approach that has something for everyone, across learning styles. But since her organization will continue to grow and change, she expects that this dynamic "best practice" for delivering research will also change.

Beyond individual styles, consider also what type of information will be most relevant to your stakeholders. You may have asked about this in your stakeholder interviews (as discussed in Chapter 1). One research team realized that results like "Users need it to be easy to clean" were too generic and not actionable by their internal customers. They evolved their process to articulate specifically what the engineers should do, with recommendations like "Surfaces should be made from elastomeric materials and all joining pieces should have no more than a 1 mm gap." Another group added a team member who was highly skilled at rapidly creating high-fidelity prototypes for developers. Research findings were translated into a prototype and then delivered in exactly the right form that the internal customer needed.

Often, you're asking people to change their minds about your users or your product. That takes some time, so collaborating with your colleagues throughout the process creates a longer—and calmer—context for them to evolve their thinking. Avoid the dramatic but ineffective "reveal" of new information and conclusions.

NOTE NOTHING SUCCEEDS LIKE SUCCESS

When you deliver research, most of the content is going to be about answering questions: the questions that you started out with and some of the questions that emerged over the course of the study. But you also may have questions that came up, which you weren't able to answer. Those questions are part of the value of the research: something to look at that you weren't even aware of previously. Striking an elegant balance between "here's what we learned" and "here's some proposals for future research" is a way for you to advocate for how research is perceived and positioned, and to have a voice in what upcoming research will be most useful to the organization.

Activated by Insights

Research frequently happens in situations where the team has long been thinking about some aspect of the product, the process, the users, and so on. You may have been in multiple meetings where the same people restate their same hopes and assumptions as facts, the same set of past (if failed) efforts are reiterated, and nothing happens. User research is powerful for breaking that cycle by bringing a clear, external point of view. It replaces opinions with insights and can change the conversation.

NOTE THE DATA IS TELLING US

Laura Faulkner, a research leader at Rackspace, developed a tactic for responding to pushback about research findings:[8] "Instead of saying 'Yeah, but the users are saying *this*' or 'We found *this* in the study'...and really starting to get our back up about that, we use that more generic research-based answer of 'Yeah, I hear you with all of those challenges...we just want you to know that the data is telling us *this*.'" Referring to the data reframes the discussion away from dueling opinions and preempts any need to debate about what action their colleagues decide to take.

FROM MY PERSPECTIVE
DON'T WAIT—DELEGATE!

I collaborated with a project manager who took the research deliverable I created and added a chart at the bottom that listed all the implications and "How might we?" questions and assigned each of them to relevant workgroups. Given the dynamics of the organization, it was perfectly appropriate (for the project manager, not for me, the consultant user researcher!) to do this. The teams all joined for a discussion of the research, but this part of the document really helped with the "Great, now what?" moment that sometimes happens. The teams weren't told what they had to do with this info, but they were pointedly asked to consider how their particular subset of insights would affect the decisions being made in their specific work streams. ▪

---

8 Steve Portigal, "28: Laura Faulkner of Rackspace," *Dollars to Donuts* (podcast), March 26, 2020, https://portigal.com/podcast/28-laura-faulkner-of-rackspace/

By Monal Chokshi

Monal Chokshi is a senior research and insights leader with over 25 years of experience. She facilitates executive decision-making through the use of insights. Monal has built and led research teams at Dropbox, Lyft, Intuit, and SoundCloud.

Doing great research is only half our job. The other half is influencing. If your insights aren't driving decision-making, you're not having the right kind of impact, no matter how great your research is. Determining *how* best to be influential in your organization is a research challenge in itself. Much of it depends on the maturity of the organization's user research practice, as well as whether or not there's an established user-centric culture where stakeholders have bought into research helping to drive decisions. Whatever the situation, you first need to put on your researcher hat to observe internal processes and then determine your best opportunities to have the most influence.

In one of my previous roles, research and insights was important but distributed. Leaders of different disciplines such as Design, Marketing, Sales, and Customer Experience/Support hired separate insights leaders to build teams for their discipline. Each of these small insights teams did a great job of partnering with their own orgs, providing them with needed insights. However, each of these insights teams remained separate and siloed from each other.

As an insights leader, one of my goals is to have a consistent, broad-reaching impact across an organization. This means not only driving decisions with teams such as Design, Product, and Marketing, but also influencing the larger business and company strategy. During my first year at this organization, I had seen our executive team begin developing our annual company strategy about six months ahead of the new fiscal year. Executive leaders approached insights teams for data to support their ideas, rather than the insights teams proactively providing executives with the necessary insights to drive their ideation and strategy decision-making. I saw an opportunity to push the envelope of what we as a collective insights community could do *together* to influence company strategy.

I formed an Insights Council, which comprised key leaders from each of the insights teams—including my team, Research and Insights (UX/Design Research and Market Insights), as well as the Data Science, Customer Experience/Voice of Customer, Competitive Intelligence, and Pricing and Packaging insights teams. Our key goal was to provide a shared perspective and a "single voice of truth" for the company. I planned an Insights Summit, a "meeting of the minds" from all of these teams, to result in a report aimed at influencing our overall company strategy and to help drive our annual planning.

This was a risky initiative, as it was not asked for, required the participation of folks from several teams, and would be seen as a waste of precious time and resources if not successful. Resources were tight for all of our insights teams, and leaders were understandably hesitant to commit their team members to a "nonessential" project that fell outside of their org's roadmap. I needed to capitalize on my strong relationship with each leader and asked for the minimal commitment. We all needed to prioritize how we used our limited resources. I assured the other leaders that no net new research would be required. The Insights Summit would utilize our already existing data and insights from prior research, and our efforts would be focused on triangulating this work to form our single voice of truth.

Over a kick-off meeting and two workshops, representatives from each team shared and discussed the most prominent insights and themes from the research they had done over the last year. Together, we crafted a shared perspective. We identified five key areas of opportunity for the company—four of which the company had already started to act upon, and one area which the company didn't have much of a line of sight into. We chose to highlight this new area as a key opportunity for our company strategy.

I had hired a vendor to help with the program management and to do an initial report, made up of contributions from across the Insights Summit participants. As a key audience for this report was executives with little time, we created strong Executive Summary and Conclusion sections, with links to each referenced report so that folks from across the company could dig into details, as desired.

We delivered the report exactly six months before the new fiscal year, which was perfect timing to provide our executives with the fuel they needed to strategize. As a result, our very first Insights Summit had a huge impact on the company strategy for the following fiscal year. By bringing together research we had already done, our report drove key objectives across the company, including our company's annual strategy, business unit strategy narratives and goals, as well as the strategies of various executives. This consolidated insights report now serves as a reference for anyone interested in our large opportunities to improve our customers' experiences and has been especially valuable for new executives and all employees who are onboarding to the company. Due to this success, we landed more resources and budget to continue this initiative on an annual basis. Executives await this report (now done biannually) to charge up their ideas and discussions around future strategy and planning.

Driving Interest and Engagement

Researchers often put in a tremendous effort to create awareness of their findings and recommendations. Some of their tactics are unique to their organizational culture and wouldn't sit right in another company, but overall, these examples should give you permission to be creative and experiment to get even better engagement.

Mailchimp built a marketing function into their user research team,[9] where their responsibility was to raise awareness and engage people. They designed team jackets with badges, DJed an in-house radio show with a usability-checklist-inspired playlist, plastered the office with playful 1980s-themed posters to promote the radio show, created a bingo card with presentation keywords, and so on.

In the past, LinkedIn ran a regular "Field Day" event where researchers took colleagues out into the field to get some basic exposure to different types of LinkedIn users. When someone completed four Field Days, they were presented with a LinkedIn lab coat (see Figure 10.3) as a positive and light-hearted acknowledgment. The lab coat might sit in the recipient's workspace where other people would ask about it, spreading a positive story about user research.

FIGURE 10.3

LinkedIn's fanciful "lab coat" reward for participating in Field Day helped create awareness of user research.

---

9 "Multipurpose Communication & UX Research Marketing with Molly Fargotstein," *DesignOps Videoconference*, January 17, 2020, www.youtube.com/watch?v=clPOukUOuLw

Even if nothing else, those efforts at LinkedIn and Mailchimp served to highlight the existence of user research. That serves as inspiration to make your process visible. For example, when a client couldn't get a meeting room for a massive fieldwork debriefing, he took over the kitchen area. Many people walked by and peeked in, intrigued to see what was happening. In some contexts, that is a crucial element in building up the practice.

Beyond that, you can increase the visibility of your outputs. Look for as many possible audiences and venues to share your results. One of my clients took the deliverable we developed together and gave 30 presentations over a few months. Another team mounted an ever-growing number of user profile posters on the walls around their workspace (see Figure 10.4).

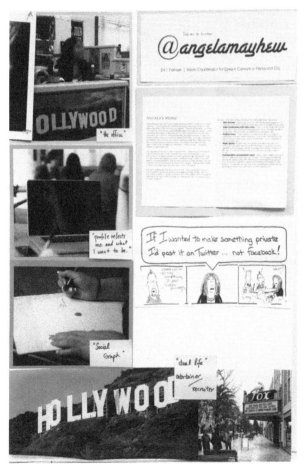

FIGURE 10.4
Field teams created profile posters, telling an engaging, visual story about an individual customer. The accumulated set of posters in the user research team's workspace raised awareness of that team's role.

Another researcher working on medical equipment did his prototyping at his desk instead of in a lab, and he found that coworkers stopped by to investigate his progress. An American client of mine built a "museum" from our research in Japan that included miscellaneous consumer items and household equipment, pamphlets and advertisements, photographs, and printed pages from our research report. This display was in place for over a year and prompted conversations for years beyond that.

Each Organization Has Its Own Challenges

A user research maturity model is a tool for examining the state of the user research practice in an organization (or perhaps, different departments). Chris Avore's model[10] (see Table 10.2) considers the following attributes of how research is conducted or received:

- **Executive attitude** (Unconvinced? Expected? Excited?)
- **Scope** (e.g., What does research cover? What are some of the methods that are being used? How far does research reach in the organization?)
- **Purpose** (e.g., Why is the organization investing in research?)
- **Staffing** (e.g., Who makes up the research team?)
- **Audience** (e.g., Who uses the findings?)
- **Governance** (e.g., What are the policies about how research will be conducted and consistently applied across teams, projects, and the organization?)

The model characterizes what you might expect to see for those attributes, depending on how mature an organization is, from Laggard through Early, Progressing, and Mature.

You can use a maturity model like this to assess the situation in your organization, facilitate conversations about the opportunities, and choose how to approach making improvements. You have to also consider the organization's strategy and the maturity of your product offerings.

---

10 Chris Avore, "The Organization's Design Research Maturity Model," *UX Collective* (blog), May 21, 2016, https://uxdesign.cc/the-organizations-design-research-maturity-model-b631471c007c

TABLE 10.2 USER RESEARCH MATURITY

	Laggard	Early	Progressing	Mature
Exec Attitude				
Scope				
Purpose				
Staffing				
Audience				
Governance				

Try to identify allies who will advocate for the kind of research you want to do. You may find newly hired leaders who believe in certain best practices from previous jobs, or isolated designers and researchers elsewhere in the corporation who are looking for their own peers and champions, or managers who know there must be a better way to reach users but don't know where to start. Reach out to the professional community for mentors, inspiration, and peer support, and to benchmark your successes against others.

As an individual, look for ways to position yourself in your organization so that interviewing customers is an integral part of how you work. If this wasn't part of your arrangement upon being hired, you need to evolve your brand with your managers and colleagues. If you can't do that, consider your future in that organization.

If you are getting pushback about interviewing users, identify the objection and target your proposal accordingly. If you're being told that the team already knows what they need to design, is that true? If so, why haven't previous initiatives succeeded? Take time to understand the problem you are being asked to solve. What has already been tried? What worked and what didn't work? Base your recommendations on that context. You aren't asking for permission here: you are making a case for solving their problem.

If there is concern about resources, be aware of what it takes to do this sort of research, and if you want to tighten the deadlines, consider—and make sure that your stakeholders understand—all of the trade-offs of doing so (see Figure 10.5). Sometimes resistance to committing resources is based on naïve assumptions about what is necessary (such as, "We have to see every type of customer.").

Your expertise in project planning will help scope the project appropriately. Determine the research needs and propose the right size project that will address them, highlighting costs and trade-offs.

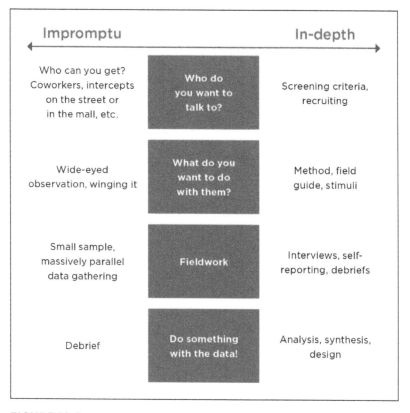

FIGURE 10.5

Consider the trade-offs that arise when deciding the amount of time and effort committed to any stage of a research project.

DOLLARS TO DONUTS

Dollars to Donuts (Figure 10.6) is my intermittently active podcast. It has featured interviews with people who lead research in their organizations, reflecting on their own journeys and the process of building the research capability in those organizations. Episodes are at **http://portigal.com/ podcast**, or just about wherever you get your podcasts. ■

FIGURE 10.6

The *Dollars to Donuts* podcast features conversations with user research leaders.

The Last Word

While we often explain that a main goal of user research is to provide information that impacts action the business takes, it's also true that creating impact can require busy people with a lot of momentum to pause, reflect, and then change their minds. You can't induce someone to adopt a new point of view, but it's within your power to create helpful conditions for that change.

- Establish a mechanism for tracking what research has been done and what you've learned.

- Since you can't do every possible research study, decide how you'll prioritize when there's too much to do.

- Consider the different individuals you want to influence to take action and where to focus your efforts.

- If your organization is resistant to interviewing users, identify the types of resistance you are facing, from cultural to resource (or other). Develop your response appropriately.

- Be creative in creating awareness, whether it's about the existence of research or about specific insights and implications for different teams.

- Nothing succeeds like success. Leverage every bit of research you do to create opportunities for more research.

- Assess your own organization's user research maturity and prioritize where to push for evolution.

INDEX

M

Mailchimp, research promotions, 236

making up interviewing methods, 72

MangoTech, field highlights, 204

mapping, as interviewing method, 59–60

Marchese, David, 179

market research, and user research, 15, 91

market research facility, interviews in, 14, 173

Maron, Marc, 155–156, 179

Mars, Roman, 130

maturity model for user research, 238–239

MediaMaster, 67

meditation, 103, 181

meltdown, 172

methods, defined, 54

methods in interviewing, 53–73

 card sort, 65–66

 concept formats, 66–69

 concept reactions, 61–63

 exercises, 60

 homework and prework, 54–56

 image cards, 64–65

 making up methods, 72

 mapping, 59–60

 observation and shadowing, 69–71

 participatory design, 60–61

 prototypes, 64, 66–67

 showing and telling, 56–58

microphones

 for audio recording, 191–192

 for video recording, 196–197

(mis)interpretations in the interview, 187

mistakes, learning from, 180

Mixed Methods (Ladner), 190

mixed methods (of research), 16

mobile phones and devices. *See* smartphones

model release, in participant release, 39

Moore, Lindsay, 168

multitasking, with cell phone during interview, 108

N

"The Naked Face" (Gladwell), 120–121

National Center on Disability and Journalism, 37

New Yorker participants, and silence, 135–136

Nokia Research Center, 59, 68–69

nondisclosure agreements (NDA), 39, 89

nonlinguistic information, 140–141, 190

nonverbal interjections, 132–134

note-taking, documenting the interview, 186–191

 descriptive, not interpretive, 191

 (mis)interpretations, 187

 for podcasting, 188–189

 typing vs. writing, 190–191

 visual note-taking (sketchnoting), 198–199

O

observation, as interviewing method, 69–72

observation guide, 71

observation skills, development of, 71

online platforms, in remote research, 83

open-ended questions, 78, 130–131

open tagging, 211–213

operational skills for researchers, 27–29, 43–45

order effects, in asking questions, 141–144

P

pain points, 5

Palovak, Jewel, 134

panel (research participants), 35

paragraphs, people speaking in, 134

paralinguistic information, 140–141, 190

participant questions, in research plan, 18

participant releases, 39–40, 89–91, 112

participants

multiple, in the interview, 175–177

priming with homework assignment, 54–55

respect for their expertise, 107

using their language, 149–151

participants, finding and recruiting, 28–37

getting participants, 35

inviting people to participate, 36–37

recruiting challenges, 36

sample criteria, 29–31

sample size, 32–33

screener (screening questions), 33–34

who you learn from and who you build for, 30–31

participants as problems

disinterested, 116–118

disrespectful, 111–112

interruptions not allowed, 174

not the right kind of user, 161–162

not truthful, 165–166

reticent, 160–161

won't stay on topic, 165

won't stop talking, 162–164

participatory design, 60–61

Paul, Joyce Kakariyil, 169–171

personal attacks, 112, 168

personal identifiable information (PII), 28, 41

photographs, documenting the interview, 49, 198

physical mock-up, 68–69

podcast interviews, note-taking for, 188–189

POEMS (People, Objects, Environments, Messages, Services), 70

power-sharing agreement, 93

practice, to improve as an interviewer, 178

pre-interview briefing, 107–108

presumptions

asking questions when you think you know the answer, 106–107

probing without presuming, 146

prework, in interview process, 54–56

process improvement, as operational skill for researchers, 45

product lifecycle, research across, 16

professional interviews (B2B), compared with consumer interviews (B2C), 175

project management, as operational skill for researchers, 44

protocol. *See* interview guide

prototypes, 64, 66–67, 238

PwDR (people who do research), 28, 29

Q

quantitative survey, 14

quantitative user experience research (quant UXR), 17

questions. *See also* asking questions

follow-up, 142–144

how might we (HMW), 219–220

kick-off, in interview, 94

listening by asking, 120

multiple-choice, 131

never say never, 82

open-ended, 78, 130–131

to participants, 18

research question, in research plan, 10–12

research repositories (knowledge management), 29, 45, 225, 227

research requests, prioritizing resources, 228–231

    hierarchy with tiers, 230–231

    stakeholders in segmentation model, 230

    worksheet/template, 228–229

research results, delivering, 218–219

research scoping, as operational skill for researchers, 44

Research That Scales (Towsey), 29

resources

    prioritizing, 228–231

    trade-offs in scoping the research, 239–240

Richards, Keith, 100

Rohrer, Christian, 14–15

role-playing, 57–58

rolling research, 8–9

rookie interviewers, 76

Rosenburg, Amanda, 231

Rosenstein, Aviva, 228

Rothman, Joshua, 130

Roviglioni, Raffaella, 168

Ruskin, Mollie, 22

S

safe spaces for interviewer and participant, 111–112

safety, danger and feeling unsafe, 166–168, 169–171

Salesforce, 225

samples of participants

    criteria for, 29–31

    inclusive research sampling, 32

    size of sample, 32–33

Santiago, Neil, 83, 84

satisficing, 5, 7

saturation, 32

scheduling interviews, 38–40

scope growth, 22

scoping the research

    considering trade-offs of resources, 239–240

    as operational skill for researchers, 44

    project scope and safety considerations, 171

screener document, 33–34, 161–162

seating, in an interview, 88–89

secondary research, 13

self-documentation, by participants, 55

sentimental data, 17

Sesame Workshop, 90

sexist language, 112, 168

Shade, Lynn, 135–137

shadowing, 69–70

'sharing,' as recruitment specification, 162

showing and telling, 56–58

Shut Up! (SU), 132

silence

    asking questions, 129–132

    cultural differences, 135–137

    improv show, and body language, 139–140

    power of, 134

Simon, Herbert, 5

The Simpsons (TV show), 140

site visits, 3

sketches, to document the interview, 198–200

sketchnoting, 198–199

small talk, 90–91, 113–114

smart home, 72–73

ACKNOWLEDGMENTS

I have so many people to thank for their kind and thoughtful help in bringing this book into the world.

The team at Rosenfeld Media, especially Marta Justak, Danielle Foster, and Lou Rosenfeld, advised, challenged, and encouraged me. My (fiction) writing instructors Ron Darian, Merrill Feitell, and David Schweidel and my (fiction) writing groups guided me on my path to being a better writer.

Dave Hora, Janelle Ward, and Tom Williams reviewed a draft of this book, offering a range of insightful perspectives and possibilities.

A whole heap of lovely people helped out with information, answers to questions, referrals, permission, content, or something else of value. For sure I'm forgetting someone, so I preemptively apologize for the omission, but can at least thank Alba Villamil, Alisa Weinstein, Allana Wooley, Amanda Rosenburg, Ayo Animashaun, Brigitta Norton, Bruce McCarthy, Cassini Nazir, Chelsey Glasson, Chris Geison, Chris Marmo, Christina Wodtke, Dan Berlin, Gabriel Trionfi, Gregg Bernstein, Irith Williams, Jake Burghardt, Jamika Burge, Jerome Axle Brown, Jorge Arango, Joyce Kakariyil Paul, Justin Threlkeld, Karri-Pekka Laakso, Kate Towsey, Kathryn Campbell, Kitty Z Xu, Lena Blackstock, Lynn Shade, Martina Hodges-Schell, Michael Margolis, Mike Gorgone, Mike Oren, Monal Chokshi, Nadyne Richmond, Noel Franus, Oren Friedman, Peter Merholz, Rebecca Buck, Reg Murphy, Sam Ladner, Sarah E. Smith, Shanae Chapman, Shannon Stoll, Shima Houshyar, Sinéad Davis Cochrane, Ted Frank, and Victor Udoewa.

I had a big mess o' people to thank in the first edition of *Interviewing Users*, and even if they don't get specifically name-checked here, I still remember and appreciate their contribution.

I'm grateful for the always reliable support and good humor from my family: Anne, Sharna, Cheryl, Bruce, Saul, Ari, Tom, and Sally.

And lastly, in the 10 years since the first edition of *Interviewing Users* was published, I've been on the receiving end of a supersized portion of acclaim and enthusiasm from people who read the book, recommended the book, gave out copies to their clients, colleagues, students, and mentees; people who to my unceasing astonishment identified themselves as "fans!" At the risk of descending into treacly boasting, I must acknowledge how meaningful and sustaining this has been for me. It serves as a reminder to me (and that I share with you) that telling someone you enjoy or appreciate their work is almost always a Very Good Thing to do.

 Rosenfeld®

Dear Reader,

Thanks very much for purchasing this book. There's a story behind it and every product we create at Rosenfeld Media.

Since the early 1990s, I've been a User Experience consultant, conference presenter, workshop instructor, and author. (I'm probably best-known for having cowritten *Information Architecture for the Web and Beyond*.) In each of these roles, I've been frustrated by the missed opportunities to apply UX principles and practices.

I started Rosenfeld Media in 2005 with the goal of publishing books whose design and development showed that a publisher could practice what it preached. Since then, we've expanded into producing industry-leading conferences and workshops. In all cases, UX has helped us create better, more successful products—just as you would expect. From employing user research to drive the design of our books and conference programs, to working closely with our conference speakers on their talks, to caring deeply about customer service, we practice what we preach every day.

Please visit 🐘rosenfeldmedia.com to learn more about our **conferences**, **workshops**, **free communities**, and **other great resources** that we've made for you. And send your ideas, suggestions, and concerns my way: louis@rosenfeldmedia.com

I'd love to hear from you, and I hope you enjoy the book!

Lou Rosenfeld,
Publisher

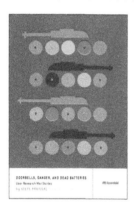

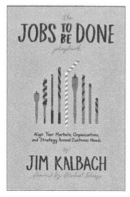
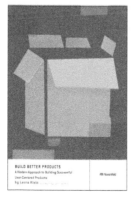

ABOUT THE AUTHOR

Steve Portigal is an experienced user researcher and consultant who helps organizations build more mature user research practices. Over the past 25 years, he has interviewed hundreds of people, including families eating breakfast, film production accountants, hotel maintenance staff, architects, realtors, home-automation enthusiasts, credit-default swap traders, and rock musicians. He has informed the development of commercial lighting controls, medical information systems, professional music gear, wine packaging, design systems, work-from-home practices, financial services, corporate intranets, videoconferencing systems, and music streaming services.

Steve is the author of two books: this one (first edition), and *Doorbells, Danger, and Dead Batteries: User Research War Stories*. He's also the host of the *Dollars to Donuts* podcast, where he interviews people who lead user research in their organizations. Steve is an in-demand presenter who gives talks and leads workshops at corporate events and conferences around the world.

He built one of the first online communities (Undercover, a Rolling Stones fan group) in 1992, nurturing it from a time when the internet was an underground academic technology through to today.

After growing up near Toronto, Steve eventually made his way to the San Francisco Bay Area where he's been for more than 25 years. He lives in the coastal town of Montara with his partner Anne and their silly dog Ripley. Steve loves to travel and eat interesting food and to take pictures of travel and interesting food. He also really loves to nap.

You can find Steve at portigal.com.

Printed in the USA
CPSIA information can be obtained
at www.ICGtesting.com
JSHW071341150424
61202JS00024B/625